Angel Standing By

Angel Standing By

THE STORY OF JEWEL

P.J. McFarland

ST. MARTIN'S GRIFFIN ❧ NEW YORK

Author's Note

The quotes from Jewel interspersed throughout this book were taken from a wide variety of published interviews she has given. I did not have the opportunity to interview Jewel myself. Dialogue has been reconstructed based on the recollection of one of the participants.

Design by Victoria Kuskowski

Library of Congress Cataloging-in-Publication Data

McFarland, P. J.
    Angel standing by : the story of Jewel / P.J. McFarland.
    p.   cm.
    ISBN 0-312-19827-2
    1. Jewel, 1974– 2. Singers—United States—Biography. I. Title.
    ML420.J38 M35   1999
    782.42164'092—ddc21
    [b]   98-44407
                                                             CIP
                                                             MN

First St. Martin's Griffin Edition: January 1999

10 9 8 7 6 5 4 3 2

Prologue

And when you cry I'll be right there
Telling you
You were never anything less than beautiful
So don't you worry
I'm your angel standing by . . .

Does anyone believe in magic anymore? As we approach the end of the century, American culture has become mired in cynicism and irony, with hope tossed by the wayside. Our role models—from athletes to entertainers to politicians—are increasingly imperfect, reflecting the cracks that have developed in our moral granite. Even the pursuit of the American Dream seems less than a legitimate ideal these days. Our pop stars especially have become antiheroes instead of heroes, reminders of hopelessness and pain. What did Kurt Cobain represent? Courtney Love? Nothing life-affirming, that's for sure.

Which makes the story of Jewel Kilcher all the more remarkable. The twenty-four-year-old Alaska native is the antithesis of all these things. She is admired for all the right reasons. She simply followed her passion for music, and it's paid off. And not just for her. Sure, her debut CD, *Pieces of You*, has sold more than eight million copies since its 1995 release. But Jewel's life has been an inspiration, a sign that good things can still happen when you follow your dream. Her success helps give us all the strength to believe that we, too, don't have to settle or compromise in our lives; that if we believe in ourselves, our possibilities are limitless.

Hers is a great American story, a postmodern Horatio Alger—from an isolated childhood in Alaska to multiplatinum success. And, really, her life is just beginning.

It was barely half over, but 1997 was already shaping up as a remarkable year for women in music, as they dominated the pop charts like never before. Yet the significance went far beyond impressive sales figures.

Certainly, women performers had struck a nerve with the culture at large in the past, most recently during the Courtney Love–led Riot Grrrl phenomenon. But this time it was different. It wasn't about dressing up as a baby doll, spewing vitriol, and being outrageous. Instead, it was about hope and independence, empowerment and possibilities—without hiding behind a mask of anger. This was all about joy and celebration.

Women were boldly chasing their dreams—and they were becoming heroes and role models. And it wasn't only the pop stars. Women athletes, authors, filmmakers, and politicians were achieving greater success than ever before.

It was nothing short of a revelation—or maybe a revolution—for girls and women everywhere who could now close the doors to their bedrooms, turn out the lights, and turn on their soundtracks to a magical world that, for a change, was within reach. Pumping up the volume on their CD players, girls could dream their Wonder Woman dreams to the assertive yet accessible melodies and words of Meredith Brooks, the Spice Girls, Paula Cole, Sheryl Crow, Alanis Morissette, Fiona Apple, and a slew of others. Believe it: Girl Power was rocking the world.

Once upon a time, Jewel Kilcher dreamed her own little-girl dream, and it came true. A talented yet culturally naive twenty-four-year-old who spent her formative years in a speck on the map—Homer, Alaska, population 4,133—Jewel didn't know any better, which probably worked to her advantage. No one told her of the folly of her dreams, or about limitations, long odds, and compromise. So she let her passion lead her—writing songs, performing her heart out—and let the chips fall. Now she's Cinderella living on a clock that will never strike midnight. Due to the dogged persistence from her label, Atlantic Records, and the determination of the artist herself, Jewel has become the It Girl for the Year of the Woman, on the cover of virtually every magazine in America. And for good reason: Jewel is an honest-to-goodness phenomenon. Just ask *Time* magazine, which put Jewel on its cover in summer 1997 accompanied by the headline: "Jewel and the Gang: Macho Music Is Out. Empathy Is In. And the All-Female Lilith Festival Is Taking Rock's Hot New Sound on the Road." The only other pop musician to appear on a newsmagazine's cover in recent memory? Bob Dylan. That's pretty good company.

Jewel became the face of Girl Power to the eight million (so far) who've bought her debut album, *Pieces of You*. The folksy, down-to-earth, blond, surfing angel with a soaring voice and a yodel like nobody's business also had a back story that's the stuff of fairy tales.

The denouement of Jewel's dream unfolded in an appropriately dreamlike place—George, Washington. Located in Grant County, smack-dab in the center of Washington State, George is equidistant from Seattle and Spokane, surrounded by other counties named after the most powerful fathers of American history—Lincoln, Adams, Franklin. Soon, it would become known as the location of the birth of a pop mother lode.

But George is not the kind of place where you imagine people actually live. Instead, you drive through it if you're driving east on Highway 28 to get to Moses Lake; if you do stop in George and you're not getting gas, it's to visit the Gorge, a bucolic outdoor concert arena that's expansive enough to accommodate the plethora of summer rock festivals that barnstorm through the country. It may be just another shed on the summer rock circuit, but on the day after America's 221st birthday, it hosted the opening performance of the inaugural Lilith Fair, a festival conceived by musician Sarah McLachlan as a celebration of women, a counterpoint to male-dominated caravans such as Lollapalooza.

The Lilith Fair was named after Adam's legendary first wife, who was banished from Eden when she demanded equality from her mate (unlike Eve, who was created from Adam's rib, Lilith was born at God's hand, like Adam). The thirty-stop tour was a coming-out party of sorts, with a revolving band of sixty-one artists signed up to play as the tour crossed the country.

All the accoutrements of the modern rock festival were in

place at the Gorge—information and food stands, a hot sun beating down that made the random spray from a water bottle seem heaven-sent, faulty sound systems, and opening-day kinks like malfunctioning ATMs. Eleven artists performed on three stages to kick off Lilith. While McLachlan headlined the festival, it was Jewel who mesmerized the crowd.

After Suzanne Vega and Paula Cole took their turns, Jewel calmly strode toward the center of the large main stage. Although she looked beguiling in her hot-tamale getup—a spaghetti-strapped evening gown and high heels—the singer, performing solo with only an acoustic guitar, looked at first like a lost girl playing dress-up. But not for long. She used her big voice to make a crowd of thousands—mostly blissed-out women grooving around in colorful, flowing floral skirts that shimmered gently in the late afternoon breeze—feel a part of an intimate gathering. Jewel sang songs whose themes many could relate to, whether they were waiting for their Marlon Brandos or accusing their partner of cheating with another woman.

You can't fault artists if, after spending nearly three years on the road as Jewel has, they occasionally phone in a performance. But a fire burns deep within Jewel's soul, and it pushes her to perfection every time she stands before an audience. While thousands of enraptured fans gently swayed, waved, and held each other, Jewel tightly closed her eyes as if to shield herself from the dark quality of her lonesome songs—"Foolish Games," "Angel Standing By," "Who Will Save Your Soul"—and sang as if her life depended on it. It wasn't about entertainment as much as survival, each note a reminder of her difficult past.

The crowd cheered at her sassy, onstage persona, and shushed to a quiet buzz when she related stories of the bad old days, when she lived in her van, when having five dollars in her pocket made her feel rich. "Foolish Games," especially, was an emotionally draining experience for performer and audience alike, as Jewel's

5

soaring voice took off into hyperspace. She also had a few surprises up her sleeve, including a rocking version of Patti Smith's classic "Dancing Barefoot," for which Jewel strapped on an electric guitar.

Jewel left a piece of herself with the Lilith audience, opening her heart to a large gathering of strangers, and they responded in kind. It was a vibe of warmth, of love, and when she dusted off her yodel during "Chime Bells," a song she had been performing since she was a child, there was euphoric pandemonium. The sprawling Gorge suddenly seemed comfortably cozy.

Jewel's abridged thirteen-song performance was a certified triumph, the culmination of a lifetime of following her heart and of relentless road work. It was a long way from Homer, Alaska; a long way from San Diego, where as a teenage waitress Jewel ate the food left by customers so she wouldn't go hungry. All her dreams had come true.

CHAPTER ONE

Morning Song

You can't tell a whole life story, even if you've lived it. As soon as you start pulling out the pieces it looks like something else. There's a tendency to focus on the more dramatic. The natural flow of things gets lost.

—Lenedra Carroll, Jewel's mother

Alaska gets all the credit, but Payson, Utah, is the unsung birthplace of Jewel Kilcher. In a small town near the center of the state, just south of Provo, Jewel entered the world without a middle name on May 23, 1974, the second child of Atz Kilcher and Lenedra Carroll.

Jewel took her first breath during a particularly tumultuous time in America's history: the energy crisis produced long gas lines and short tempers across the nation; Richard Nixon was feeling the heat from Watergate and would resign his presidency in three short months; polyester and bell-bottoms were all the rage. Men wore their hair as long as possible, and all over their faces. The Vietnam war, televised before a gaping generation of Americans, was coming to a close.

Jack Nicholson and Faye Dunaway confronted their demons in *Chinatown;* Robert DeNiro and Al Pacino protected the Corleone family's interests in *The Godfather, Part II.* We were nostalgic for the 1950s, spending time with Richie Cunningham and his friends Fonzie, Potsie, and Ralph on *Happy Days.* David Bowie's *Diamond Dogs* was on the radio, along with Elton John's *The Bitch Is Back.*

Tellingly, Joni Mitchell was enjoying her greatest commercial success in mid-1974. Her *Court and Spark* album, with hits "Free Man in Paris" and "Help Me," was on Billboard's Top Ten the week Jewel was born. Although the young star is often compared to the legendary Canadian singer/songwriter, Jewel admits she didn't become familiar with Mitchell's music until after she'd written most of her debut album, *Pieces of You.*

Jewel wasn't long in Utah. The family, which included Jewel's parents and older brother, Shane, soon made its way north and west, across the plains and desolate territories of Canada to Alaska. They settled south of Anchorage, in the Kilcher family's 770-acre homestead, eleven miles outside the town of Homer. Soon thereafter, Jewel's younger brother, named Atz like his father, was born.

By the midseventies, most American singer/songwriters—indeed most Americans—were accustomed to modern conveniences. They flipped switches and on came the lights. They had eight-track tape players in their cars, and stereo systems in their living rooms. Some had central air-conditioning and heat. But the Kilchers were a throwback: they lived simply off their land, without running water or electricity. Their heat came from a coal stove that needed constant attention; for water, they relied on a pump behind their house that snaked down to a nearby stream.

When the stream flooded—and it flooded often—worms squirmed through the pump's tap. And showers? Not a chance. The Kilchers often bathed in a homemade pool they shared with their neighbors. With an ever-growing menagerie of kids and animals, the Kilchers were the twentieth-century version of the Ingalls family, living contentedly in a little house on the prairie. And Ma and Pa Kilcher were troubadours of the pioneer spirit.

Atz and Nedra had dabbled in music when living in Payson, Utah's, artistic community while also juggling academic pursuits and child-rearing, but music became more fundamental after their trek to Alaska. In fact, singing was one of the many things the clan did for its supper. There was always music, and it permeated every aspect of their lives. A meal could not be eaten without a singalong to whet the appetite.

A few years after their move from Utah, Atz and Nedra became a folksinging duo of note in America's forty-ninth state. Their songs were straightforward and honest, melodic and tied to the land. Atz and Nedra even released two albums. The first, 1977's *Early Morning Gold,* was an acoustic collection of modern Alaskan folk songs—all of which Atz had a hand in writing. 1978's *Born and Raised on Alaska Land,* more glossily produced, also featured all original material, and included a contribution from Atz's sister, Mairiis "Mossy" Davidson, who was no slouch in the songwriting department, either. Having recorded and released an album in 1977, *North Wind Calling—Mossy Davidson's Alaska,* Mossy was a popular barroom performer. Atz and Nedra became not only a popular attraction in Alaska's nightclubs, lounges, and dinner theaters, with a reputation known far and wide, they were credited with creating the first real Alaskan folk music.

Twenty years after the recording of those albums, Atz Kilcher remains such an important part of Alaska's musical fabric that he will never be known merely as the father of Jewel. In fact, up there it's the other way around. Atz is considered something of a state treasure—a top-notch entertainer, songwriter, and storyteller. Teaching music at elementary schools in and around Homer, Atz is a keeper of Alaska's cultural flame. In an era of information overload, where bits and pieces of data fly by us at hyperspeed, he is a reminder that one's heritage is important, something to be maintained and passed to future generations. It is a lesson his daughter learned well.

* ⋆ *

The Kilcher family had actually planted roots in Alaska a generation earlier. Jewel's grandparents arrived in the territory from Switzerland in 1941, amid the chaos of World War II. They settled in Homer, a blip of a town, but one of great beauty, with its majestic snowcapped mountains, glaciers, fjords, and ample wildlife. Millions of birds migrate to Kachemak Bay each year, soaring over moose and bears, lakes and streams, and Cook Inlet, where many halibut swim. Indeed, locals call Homer the halibut capital of the world.

Beginning as a place where coal and gold miners looked to strike it rich in the late nineteenth century, Homer was more of a bust than a boomtown for its first settlers. The community got its name from one of its early dreamers, Homer Pennock, who recognized its rich beauty and wealth of resources. The sheer gorgeousness of the region has made an impression on settlers the world over. It was known as Summerland by the Russians because of its lushness during the temperate months. The Aleuts along the Alaskan Peninsula called it Smoking Bay, thanks to the legacy of the coal miners. The Alaskan Chamber of Commerce's description, though, says it all: Shangri-la. "Because nowhere else in the forty-ninth state do all the elements of Alaskan beauty come together quite so felicitously." Jewel calls Kachemak Bay her favorite place in the world.

Yule Kilcher came to Shangri-la to create a better life for his family. He settled 320 acres on Kachemak, and as he hand-cleared hundreds of acres of the land by himself, the homestead steadily grew. Yule was, and still is, a tireless worker on the land. He was determined to hunker down in his new country, possessing the do-anything-to-succeed attitude that was common of emigrants leaving Europe during the first half of the twentieth century. And, like many immigrant families of the period, the Kilchers were a large clan. In all, Yule and his wife Ruth had eight children: Mairiis, Wurtila, Fay, Sunrise, Otto, Stellavera, Catkin, and Atz.

Like many of Homer's early settlers, Jewel's paternal grandfather was also a dreamer, with a streak of fearlessness and invincibility. There's nothing, he thought, that a human being couldn't do if only he'd give it a try. More than a little of Jewel's undeniable drive came from her grandfather's example. In fact, when Alaska applied for statehood, Yule wanted to have a hand in Alaska's destiny, so he became a local political force, and got elected to the state senate. In 1959, when Alaska was admitted as the forty-ninth state in the union, he was among the primary authors of its constitution. A renaissance man in every way, he made a film about life on the homestead, which he took on the road, conducting lecture tours throughout the U.S. and in Europe about living off the land. And he still hasn't slowed down. If you're ever in Homer, be careful he doesn't run you over as he tools through town in a horse and buggy, which he uses to get around when his car isn't running.

Yule—like the Kilchers who followed him—was trained in all things artistic. The Kilchers' settlement was isolated, far from town, and by turning their attention to artistic pursuits, the family could lose themselves in a magical, self-contained world of boundless creativity. They were making music, but also weaving, carving, writing, and painting. It certainly kept the growing clan occupied.

But Yule did more than simply instruct his family about the joys of music and art. With Ruth by his side, he barnstormed across Alaska and the continent, singing about the pleasures of nature and melting the crowds lucky enough to hear him. His was an era where if you wanted a house you built it yourself, and if you liked music you played and sang it yourself. He instilled in his children, and in those he met in his travels, the need to be artistically self-sufficient. He created culture wherever he went, and he knew instinctively that the arts created a framework whereby people could better know themselves, and better appreciate their world.

Every day was a gift to Yule and Ruth Kilcher. It was not an easy life, but the couple turned to music as a solace from the hardship of their existence. Alaska is beautiful and lush in the summertime, but can be cold and unforgiving in winter. Music took the Kilchers away from their troubles and brought them closer as a family. "Singing was always a big unifying force [in the family], no matter what other conflicts went on," Atz's sister Mossy Davidson once said. "You can't be mad at each other when you have to harmonize."

Certainly the harmonies, which were passed on to the next generation, helped distract the family from the cruel Alaskan winters they had to endure. Temperatures regularly dropped below freezing, and none of the Kilcher kids wanted to be the first to the outhouse, which had to be thawed daily. Jewel and her brothers shared a bedroom, and the trio often argued about who'd be the unlucky one to leave the warmth of their coverlet and make their outhouse stall functional in the subzero temperatures. Eventually it became a moot point for Jewel, who was often up before the sun anyway to milk the cows.

How cold was it? So cold that the coal stove meant to heat their dwelling would freeze and go out during the night. So cold that clothes would have to be thrown under the blankets before dressing could be tended to. And so cold, Jewel would recall, that every morning crystals of frost would start forming on the Kilcher kids' eyelashes.

Without TV or radio, without *Happy Days* or David Bowie or Joni Mitchell or Olivia Newton-John, without the Atari video games that had become must-haves across the continental United States, without even the attention-diverting board games and manufactured toys that kept most children occupied through their childhoods, the Kilcher children found other ways to amuse themselves. They spent their days playing outside, letting their imaginations develop and run wild. They learned that days and nights are punctuated by a setting sun and rising stars. That weather travels with the wind. That the color of leaves is as reliable a calendar as any hanging on the wall. "A lot of kids grow up knowing how to bank, but I'm a retard about city things," Jewel has said about her early years in Homer. "But I know what a porcupine sounds like climbing a tree."

The wilds of Homer were not only Jewel's playground, they were her first classroom. It wasn't until fourth grade that Jewel attended public school. In the years before, during the harsh winter months, Atz often took his three children to the edge of a nearby canyon, where they'd listen to the wind and the rustle of leaves and branches. God's music. Sometimes they'd dig at the sides of the cliff, exposing the frozen willow roots. Then they'd dig up the roots and weave them into baskets. Jewel learned how trees grew, from roots to trunk to branches to leaves. She learned that plants and animals are born, and live, and die. She could name the flowers and the trees, and she learned about the "birds and the bees" and about the difference between the sexes—not from textbooks, but by watching animals breed. It was an education in real life. Jewel realized knowledge could be gleaned at every turn. Freed from the restrictions of textbooks, Jewel felt unencumbered, able to open and trust the creative side of her mind at a tender age.

The amount of work required to maintain the homestead, sowing and reaping, milking and feeding, helped Jewel develop a strong sense of discipline, as well as a superhuman work ethic. This enabled her as an adult to do the work required for success as an entertainer. It was her mother's artistic training, however, that gave Jewel her first lessons on what it takes to be a musician. Nedra worked as a glass sculptor during Jewel's early childhood, and was relentless in imposing her attitudes about the creative process; growing up became one giant workshop for Jewel and her brothers about maintaining and utilizing artistic resources and instincts. By the time Jewel was five, Nedra was providing creative challenges to her children, like the poetry workshops she conducted for her little ones the first Monday of every month. Days became filled with ideas and thoughts and observations. Among the concepts Nedra taught her kids was the connection of things that offered a similar emotional response even though the things weren't necessarily similar. When Jewel realized this was the case with lambs and clouds, it became the subject of one of her earliest poems. Jewel was hooked: a writer at age five.

Even before she was writing poetry, though, Jewel was riding horses. As a young child she had her own horse named Clearwater, who turned out to be a loyal companion for the young girl, and a great mode of transportation, especially during the snowy winters, when she often rode him to school. Jewel and Clearwater were inseparable. Only on Clearwater could she have moved so swiftly through thickets and trees and experienced the wilds of nature as if she were an integral part of it. While other kids waited impatiently for learner's permits, Jewel was a "licensed driver" before she could read. Clearwater was her best friend. They were beautiful together.

In truth, though, nobody thought Clearwater would survive when the Kilchers adopted him. He was seriously ill and Jewel's parents believed he had little chance of living. The horse wouldn't eat. Atz and Nedra worried that Jewel might get too attached to her new pet, only to experience the pain of losing him. But Jewel refused to accept that Clearwater wouldn't survive. He just couldn't die—it wasn't possible. Jewel gathered bales of hay and stayed with the animal day and night. She wouldn't give up until her horse began to eat. And, eventually, he did. Purposeful even as a young child, Jewel somehow nursed him back to health. Even then, Jewel had the power to heal.

The Kilchers weren't a religious family in the conventional sense. They had been Mormons for a period of Jewel's youth, but gradually embraced a broader, less dogmatic spirituality. Atz was a social worker at that time, and helping others became a religion in itself. And besides, as Jewel said, "Being raised in Alaska on an eight-hundred-acre homestead, you just felt godliness around you. And that you were part of it. It was more about innocence and enlightenment than control." One need only listen to her song "Painters" to understand that Jewel's religion is based on a quest for knowledge about things larger than herself. The sky, for example, or the mountains, or the large open spaces of her home state.

These spaces also made her aware of the power of dreams. She'd bask in the immensity of the silence around her. In silence, she has said, "You create yourself . . . you hear who you're going to become." To this day, Jewel travels with mementos of her youth in Homer. Along with photographs and other memories, she keeps a jar of earth to remind her of her roots.

In fourth grade, when Jewel joined other children in public school, she had a far stronger background in the arts, sciences, music, and philosophy than other children. This made her something of a cultural misfit, perhaps, but it prepared her for the life she would be forced to live years later—a life in which she acted as an example to others.

Jewel learned about adversity early in her school life. She had been a good, eager learner at home. She had enjoyed and excelled at writing and drawing and sculpting. She had even seemed to read well as a child. But she encountered problems with reading soon after arriving at McNeill Canyon Elementary School. At first she thought she simply wasn't smart enough. Where other kids would fly through a passage, it would take Jewel three or four attempts. She became frustrated, and seemed to like reading less and less. It would take some time for her to understand she had dyslexia. This failed to deter her, and it ultimately made her stronger. At ten years old, Jewel was more rounded, and more talented than her peers. What she lacked as a reader, she more than made up in other ways. She was an extraordinary girl.

As early as anyone can remember, Jewel listened to music. Her first record (a tape, actually—without electricity, Jewel heard music on a portable cassette player that used batteries) aside from those in her parents' collection, turned out to have been bought accidentally. It was Pink Floyd's *The Wall*, which Jewel purchased in an Anchorage supermarket. But, as a five-year-old whose reading skills were still fairly rudimentary, she bought what she thought was a Pink Panther record. She listened to the cassette over and over again, almost wearing it out, thinking songs like "Another Brick in the Wall" and "Comfortably Numb" were being sung by a furry pink cartoon creature.

Aside from listening to the albums her parents made, whose lyrics she had memorized by her fifth birthday, Jewel developed a fascination with the legendary jazz stylist Ella Fitzgerald. Over and over Jewel would play *Ella Fitzgerald Sings the Cole Porter Songbook*, focusing not only on the words, but upon the melody, the harmonies, and how they were sung. As a small child Jewel could imitate the way Ella sang, note for note. She could fairly accurately reproduce the way Ella extended her phrases, initiated her vibrato—Jewel even had an innate understanding of the way she breathed. From the start, in her childlike way, it was a study of the jazz great, as opposed to a simple mimicry.

Jewel's mother Nedra also remembers that Jewel was always performing, dressing up, and putting on shows for her family. Jewel was a ham. Not only was she never rattled by a crowd, she was inspired by one. Though her brothers had also exhibited similar skills—they both had fine natural singing voices and also liked to perform—it was Jewel who decided to practice, to play the Cole Porter tunes over and over until she got them right. One day Nedra and Atz realized that little Jewel knew their entire repertoire. She was a sponge, it seemed, with endless capacity. The only realistic solution was for her to join her parents' act.

Of course, brothers Shane and little Atz were also interested in performing on stage. And for a while, they did. A "homestead horn" was incorporated into the act: it was made of a hose and funnel, and both boys accompanied the proceedings by blowing heartily. But only their sister had the determination and the discipline to rehearse six hours each day. Jewel was tireless. And it turned out she was a natural on stage. By the time she was six, Jewel had become an integral part of the family's traveling show. At nightclubs throughout the state, the three Kilchers blended music, comedy, and Alaskan history as part of their evening's entertainment.

In the winter months, they performed select concerts around

the state. But during the summer, their tour became a full-time gig: six days a week for three months.

They played at hotels in southern Alaska like the Captain Cook and the Hilton. "Those days were filled with butterscotch Lifesavers bought from hotel gift shops, waiting to go on . . ." Jewel recalled. "That went on for about three years." During these caravans Jewel first learned to find her light onstage, to focus, and to concentrate in front of a crowd. Aside from the novelty of being entertained by someone so young, audiences were aware they were being sung to by an especially talented young girl. "Anything I would tell her to do with her voice, she could do," her father once said. This included yodeling. And thus, Jewel's legendary yodeling prowess was unearthed. She had learned the skill by mimicking her dad, who himself learned from listening to old cowboy records. At first, Atz thought his daughter was too young to be a yodeler. There had, after all, been no precedent for underage yodeling. In fact, a professor of music stopped them after one of their shows to tell them that what she had seen—a six-year-old yodeling—was impossible. She shouldn't have been able to yodel, since her vocal chords would not have developed enough. But real or imagined, Jewel continued to wow the crowds with her yodeling speed and technique on "Chime Bells." In truth, the hyperyodeling segment of "Chime Bells" was part of another song Atz sang to his daughter in Swedish called "The Swiss-Alaskan Yodel." Jewel melded the two together, and the crowds loved it.

By all accounts, Jewel had an idyllic life with a loving family, steeped in culture and music. She was happy performing with her parents in front of appreciative crowds. She was meeting people from all over the world.

Then the band broke up. Her father and mother, who had seemed so happy from the viewpoint of a small child, decided to call it quits. Divorce came between Atz and Nedra Kilcher, and Jewel remembers her father "leaving [her] mom on a street corner while [they drove] away in the back of a car." Jewel moved in with her father, and suddenly the family act became a duo.

CHAPTER TWO

From Roots to Wings

*I constantly skip around my hotel room going, I'm a writer.
That's what I do. I write.*

Jewel's perfect little world changed drastically. She learned the reason for her parents' divorce over an evening meal, while seated at the family's dinner table. As Jewel later recounted in the nakedly autobiographical song "Nikos," her father had been with a woman named Linda, a divorcée who lived nearby in a trailer on Eastern Road, and Linda had become pregnant. When Jewel looked him in the eye, Atz cast his eyes downward.

Some time later, according to the songs, while Jewel was living with her father, she was called to the principal's office. There, she was handed a telephone and suddenly was speaking to a doctor. "You've got a baby brother," he told her. Though she tried to hold it in, Jewel admits in "Nikos" to being "bitter in my anguish," and recounts that she was sent to a psychiatrist "in case I resented the child" and that her father was excommunicated from the Mormon church.

Jewel's father may have hoped to play a larger role in the newborn's life than he would be allowed. The child was named Nikos, and Atz "could see him on every other Saturday." Linda married another man who insisted that Nikos call him Dad, and that he call Atz Uncle. Shortly thereafter, the marriage went sour. Through this period, Atz and Linda tried to work things out between them, but to no avail. Eventually Linda left Homer and relocated to Oregon.

Jewel's reaction to her parent's divorce was not much different than that of any other child, except that it became a matter of extremes: once the adorable little ham of the family, Jewel turned inward. She suddenly became withdrawn and confused. Her abundant self-confidence was shattered. It was a shocking, eye-opening experience for the eight-year-old. It was as though she had been in a warm, fuzzy slumber her entire life, only to be awakened by a nightmare turned real.

As she struggled to make sense of her parents' split, a large chunk of Jewel's youthful innocence was stripped away. Still, along with that loss of innocence came a self-reliance she had never before utilized. Her life up to this point, even her artistic life, had been an exercise in collaboration with others. Her singing had been a contribution to the family's act. Her desire to help Clearwater recover from his ills was an attempt to help another soul—albeit the soul of a horse. Now she found herself alone.

Nedra and Atz were given joint custody of the three children, but they all remained with Atz in Homer. This decision was made by both parents. Atz had family in Homer, and Nedra would leave Homer and settle in Anchorage. It made perfect sense to keep the children at their childhood home, thereby shaking up their lives as little as possible. It also took the heat off the kids, who were in too much a state of shock to take sides, let alone make choices. They loved both of their parents. "I couldn't have chosen. None of us could choose. It's unthinkable," Jewel has said.

She has compared her parents' divorce to having the air she breathed taken away from her, as though she suddenly found herself tossed into a strange and unfamiliar climate. Gradually, though, Jewel's anger turned to acceptance, largely because she took to heart the lessons her parents taught about channeling pain and adversity into art. Pain, Jewel was told at a young age— and now experienced firsthand—was a part of life. An irrevocable part.

Faults, she learned, are human. And so the pressure she placed upon herself—first, to repent for causing her parents' divorce; second, to help them reunite; and third, to understand it all—slowly eased. They eased as Jewel began to write things down. She started a journal and wrote poems. Writing became, she said, "My link to what was real and what I knew was sincere inside myself." Implicitly she understood the notion that, as Annie Dillard has said, "We write to find out what we know." Along with this thinking came the realization that writing, like discovery, is an ongoing process—and not a result. "It started to become a third limb or a sixth sense with me." Soon, Jewel could lose herself in her poems and journals, crawling inside and curling up with her thoughts, finding a comfortable place to dwell.

Poetry, especially, forced Jewel to deal with her feelings of abandonment and confusion. These feelings would have been unbearable without fighting back with the most powerful weapons she could lay her hands on: pencil and paper. Through writing she confronted her fears, her joys, and perhaps most important, what was really true or false. "Writing makes you more intimate with yourself," Jewel said. "It is also to this day my best friend and greatest freedom."

Her early writing, although surely naive, was always focused, such as in "Nikos," which is written like a letter to her baby half-brother. Rather than have her verses hang in a void, as mere childish screamings to the winds, Jewel had already acquired the technique of directing her voice in a linear narrative. Her song was for the child, intimate, sweet, sincere:

"This song is for Nikos wherever you may be
I know things were tough but you're okay by me
And your momma ain't a bad person, my daddy ain't no fool
Sometimes parents just need forgiving too
P.S. I love you, your sister Jewel."

As her writing output increased, Jewel's performance schedule also became busier. She and Atz regrouped and toured Alaska as a father-daughter duo for the better part of seven years. The trappings changed, however. Instead of the relatively plush hotel lounges she had played when the whole family performed together, her act with Dad usually took place in the smoky dusk of a saloon. Amid the noisy chaos of the bars—where the performers play second, even third fiddle to the rounds of booze and the sexual games played among the patrons—Jewel paid her showbiz dues. She began to develop poise and learned to assess, work, and finally captivate even the toughest of audiences. By the age of ten, Jewel was a barroom veteran, a professional who had witnessed a dark side of humanity that most performers are spared until adulthood.

She saw women guzzling their drinks because they were too afraid of who they were, who they had ever been, or what they would some day become. She saw men who regretted everything they'd ever done, but not enough to stop doing the same things. She saw gay men pretending to be hounds—their hands all over women's bodies—so that locals wouldn't beat them to pulps. And Jewel learned at a young age about sex and the games people play surrounding it: like "pawn[s] in a chess game," she has said. "I saw women who would compromise themselves for compliments, for flattery; or men who would run away from themselves by drinking until they ultimately killed themselves."

The sadness she saw in the glowing, pink, alcoholic faces staring up at her from those rickety stages affected her in many ways. To young Jewel, life for these people was a heartbreaking proposition—one that she would aspire never to know. Along with this realization, Jewel developed a disdain for drinking alcohol, which—in spite of the pressures—she still refuses to this day.

The stage became a home away from home, and sometimes even her first home. She was forced to forge fast relationships with her audiences and, by empathizing with them, to gain their confidence. And these "fast best friends," if only for a few hours, became important to her. She was like a kid whose family moved to a new place every year and who constantly had to meet new people under new conditions. Except that, rather than every year, Jewel did this every night. "I grew up in front of people. I never had friends my age," she said. "I was with adults all the time. I was used to people talking to me like an adult. Kid talk was very difficult for me."

At one steady gig, Jewel came to know a regular customer very well. The man had a routine: Each night he would lay his money in front of him on the stained walnut bar in piles: twenties, tens, fives, ones. Every night, there would be two pitchers of beer, sitting side by side. He'd drink the first pitcher quickly, slowing down as he moved on to the second. Midway through pitcher number two, he would request the same three songs: "Ain't Gonna Study War No More," "Cottonfields," and "House of the Rising

Sun." Always sad songs. The man would just sit there and drink, and by the end of Atz and Jewel's first set, this man would lift up his head and ask Jewel to come to the bar. "He [told] me to pick any bill I wanted. I'd always take a twenty and get a Shirley Temple with it. And he'd get hammered," Jewel once reminisced.

"One day he didn't come in." Apparently the man had gotten particularly drunk, and the barman felt it necessary to drive him home, make him a pot of coffee, and put him to bed. Once the bartender left, this sad, drunken man shot himself in the face. The man was a Vietnam veteran, a medic who, because he wasn't a doctor, was forced to kill wounded soldiers to put them out of their misery. What a story for a young girl to hear. "He didn't have any family so we gave him a fundraiser to get him a coffin."

Jewel learned a great deal from these encounters. Jewel remembered that once, while playing with Atz in an old veteran's bar, her audience was no larger or more elegant than three aging veterans missing teeth and limbs and "wasted out of their minds."

"I was in a bad mood from arguing with my dad, so I was onstage crying. My dad would say, 'Jewel, you have to leave your personal life behind when you're onstage.'" This apparently brought little solace to the young chanteuse, whose cries soon became sobs. "Then this drunk told me, 'Stop looking so goddamned depressed.'" This stopped Jewel dead in her tracks. Somehow, even at that age, she understood that she had crossed a line: the line of professionalism. Jewel has often said that, since that experience, when she performs she considers herself an entertainer, as opposed to an artist. "Now," she says, "when I get onstage, no matter what mood I'm in, I [make sure I] do a good show."

With guidance from her road-tested dad, Jewel learned to be quick on her feet and give the people what they wanted. The pair's set was usually filled with Atz Kilcher originals—Atz sang lead while Jewel helped out on harmonies and background vocals. On occasion, though, Jewel did take center stage, fielding requests nd covering songs popular on the radio at the time. Performing nearly every night gave Jewel valuable experience in developing her voice. Repetition helped her learn her range. It was no accident that by the time she began performing on San Diego's coffeehouse circuit, her voice's versatility had become the stuff of legend.

Jewel watched closely as her father prepared for the show, taking into account the vibe of the crowd. Her dad often made songs up on the spot, if it seemed appropriate—Atz Kilcher was a master at crowd handling. He was a mesmerizing storyteller, and lured his audience in with often-hilarious between-song banter. He could draw upon the day's events, stories from his youth, jokes about his daughter, or he could make witty references to events taking place in the bar. Anything was fair game to Atz: from the lovers smooching in a corner booth, to the gloriously tacky sequin dress worn by the bar owner's wife. If the crowd consisted of a bunch of inattentive drunks, Atz might turn his performance energy toward his daughter, entertaining her with off-the-cuff songs about people with beer in their ears. "[My dad] taught me that you can get your brain that loose, [and] just make up words on the spot. So now I can write songs spontaneously."

Spontaneity became a trademark of Atz and Jewel's act. The young performer took copious mental notes, and used this unscripted approach to performing when she embarked, years later, on her solo career. Atz never used a set list; neither does Jewel. She compares an audience to a live animal. "You have to read its body language, see what the mood is, and then fit each song to that sort of group consciousness."

When Jewel was twelve, after years in roadside taverns on rickety stages, she convinced her parents that it was time for her to see more of the world. So she left America's forty-ninth state to spend some time in the fiftieth. She moved to Hawaii, where she stayed with an aunt. For a girl on the verge of adolescence, especially one living in the frigid climes of Alaska, the lure of the Aloha state for Jewel was clear and undeniable. Hawaii was lined with beautiful beaches and lapping tides, where one could let grains of sparkling white sand trickle through one's toes. Then again, there was the warm climate.

But Jewel quickly found that warm temperatures don't necessarily go hand in hand with warm welcomes. Although Hawaiians, like Alaskans, can be gregarious and family-oriented, a sense of provincialism hangs over its people, an underlying bitterness that came with statehood. Thus, sometimes nonnatives who come to live on the islands are treated with suspicion—especially ones who look like blond Alaskan girls of Swiss descent. Jewel blended in with the natives as well as a dachshund in a kettle of Dobermans. And she was reminded of it every day. The island kids first ignored her entirely. Then, as they "warmed" to her, they taunted and teased her. Before long they threatened to beat her up because of the color of her hair and skin. Jewel was miserable. This abuse was far worse than the worst she took from any audience at the sleaziest Alaskan bar. Imagine the young Jewel sitting in class and dreading the ringing of the school bells, especially the last bell, which signaled that the school day was over. Imagine the trip to her locker, and from there the journey through the schoolyard, past a sea of disapproving faces. Imagine conversations ceasing as she passes them. From her twelve-year-old perspective, menace seemed to live in the faces and hearts of her schoolmates. And any attempts Jewel made to forge friendships caused her embarrassment and sadness.

Imagine, after weeks of abuse—and a resolve on her part to cope with this unpleasantness as best she could—the mostly benign grudge against her takes a more serious turn. As she makes her way through the schoolyard one day, she notices that some of the usual faces are missing. As she turns a corner, she's stopped by those very faces she's noticed were absent. Imagine them walking toward her, backing her against a wall, surrounding her. They take a few steps closer, and would certainly beat her to a pulp, except that Jewel has a strange epiphany, or perhaps she's just lucky. Rather than screaming, she yodels at the top of her lungs. The tough kids step back, shocked. Rather than continue to advance on her they simply listen, transfixed, to the white girl making this strange noise. Imagine the grimaces on the bullies' faces turning to smiles.

Jewel figured her problems were over. Actually, they were just beginning. Now that her yodeling prowess had been displayed publicly, the bullies insisted on a daily encore, threatening to beat her up if she didn't entertain them. And so Jewel yodeled to save her skin for the rest of her days in Hawaii, which were few. She stayed in Hawaii less than a year before returning to Alaska, this time to live with her mother, Nedra, in Anchorage. Soon thereafter they moved to Seward, only a couple hours by car from Homer. During that period, Jewel performed with Atz whenever she had the chance, but because of the distance and the fact that she was enrolled in school, those chances became fewer and farther between.

After returning from Hawaii, Jewel's life became more normal, and she began hanging out more with kids her own age. She fell into normal adolescent routines, such as experimenting with makeup and having crushes on boys. She also took to dressing experimentally during this time, showing up at school in forties dresses and pillbox hats, shrouding her face in black netting.

But the Alaskan kids, she discovered, could be as cruel as the kids back in Hawaii. In eighth grade, she developed a crush on a guy whom the other kids in school teased, saying he was gay. Jewel's friends began to abandon her because she was hanging out with "faggots." Even at that age, this went against every instinct she had—and everything she was taught. Eventually, Jewel confronted one of them. "I was like, 'You're just being prejudiced,'" Jewel remembered. That guy, it turned out some time later, was gay himself. Thus Jewel learned another lesson that strengthened her commitment to tolerance: We often dislike what we ourselves are, because we haven't come to accept ourselves. Years later, when Jewel introduced a black boyfriend of hers, a young man named Damien, to her father, Atz broke down and cried. When Jewel asked him what was the matter, he muttered: "I'm so proud that I raised such an open-minded daughter."

Jewel struggled with school in eighth grade. Again, she couldn't understand why she had so much trouble with the class's reading assignments. She had been an avid reader, and it frustrated her that though her mind raced and her tongue was sharp, she had trouble absorbing words as quickly from the page. "I thought, what a bummer, my passion all drained out of me." She went to a doctor, who diagnosed the thirteen-year-old with dyslexia. It floored her, to learn that she had a four-syllable problem. But really it was a relief. She embraced the corrective exercises he prescribed, and overcame the problem in her singular fashion: by staring it down and dealing with it.

The following year, Jewel was adopted by a Native American family. She had two uncles who were "huge, huge Ottawa Indians." Through them she was invited to a powwow, which she found to be a fantastic experience. One of the participants took her out to a meadow and told her that in the future she would be required to speak honestly to people. He continued by explaining to Jewel that she didn't yet know how to speak from her heart and would need to learn. The man's family took Jewel under its wing and included her in their tribal rituals, like drumming, dancing, and performing the "talking circle," where they told tales from Indian folklore. The "adoption" may have been short-lived, but its effects were not. Jewel had been having mature and complicated feelings for years, but her experience with the Native American family caused her to look inward in an attempt to have them make sense to her. Although she had been writing consistently for years, she had a long way to go before she found a way to translate her complex emotions into honesty on the page. "I remember," she says, "going on top of a mountain and trying to say anything honest—just to the wind. I was crying because I couldn't say anything sincere."

From this point on, Jewel was aware that sincerity was a serious proposition. The world is often insincere, either because people usually don't say what they mean, or they say nothing at all. Looking within, and striving for a type of rigorous honesty, she learned, was life's work. This helped her become a more special human being and, years later, helped her give her heart in the name of honesty to people the world over.

Her experience with Native American culture also opened doors to a world of philosophical possibilities. Coincidentally, her outside forays into spirituality coincided with the literature she was being assigned in school. While her ninth-grade classmates struggled through their required reading lists, Jewel had already developed an insatiable appetite for the points of view of other cultures. She happily read the work of South American poets Pablo Neruda, Octavio Paz, and Gioconda Belli. She absorbed the worldly philosophers Kant, Pascal, and Plato. Reading these writers, Jewel has said, taught her how to think. She paid particularly close attention to Plato's *Symposium* and was stirred by the idea that immortality can be achieved through love and beauty. During this period, aided by her experiences in the meadows with her uncles and their families, she contemplated what it means to die and be born again.

"I was really into it for a while," she said. "But I realized after a while that there were all these philosophers like Plato and Socrates who were willing to accept the possibility of immortality, but were unable to accept the fact that they had sexual desires or that they had to go to the bathroom. And I figured, what is truth if it's deducted [sic] through pure reason? Full truth has to be balanced with emotion and with the living world." As a young teenager, she may not have fully understood the work of these philosophers, but she did come to valuable conclusions which would remain with her to this day: namely, that kings and queens, along with rock stars and Kant and Jesus Christ and the average Joe, all have bodies they're not completely comfortable with; they use the bathroom, get hungry and full; they fall in love and have their hearts broken; they do things they shouldn't do; they have regrets and hopefully learn to get over them; they are mistreated and they are praised. Humans, Jewel learned, are indeed human. Without coming to these conclusions at an important time in her development, Jewel could never have become a songwriter capable of writing with such compassion.

Although one cannot be taught to "have a heart," it is possible to learn how to use it. There were other literary influences during this time. The lascivious sensuality of Henry Miller's *Tropic of Cancer,* and Anais Nin's *Diaries* and *Delta of Venus,* also piqued Jewel's interest. (She tipped her hat to both in a lyric for *Pieces of You's* "Morning Song.") She was still writing poetry and experimenting with the relationship between poems and song lyrics at this time. All the while, the performance bug had yet to leave the teenager. Jewel still performed with her dad, who added a friend, Suzanne Little, to their act. The trio was called New Directions. Jewel also became interested in the music of the day, and with some ninth-grade friends she joined a rap group called La Creme. Jewel's rapper name was, rather appropriately, Swiss Miss.

By sixteen, though, Jewel was feeling antsy again, eager to experience life beyond the isolation of Alaska. Anchorage began to feel small, even though she had few cities with which to compare it. She didn't quite know what she wanted to do, but she knew she wasn't yet doing it. Nedra convinced Jewel to apply to spend her junior and senior years at the Interlochen Arts Academy in Michigan, a prestigious school with a stellar international reputation for training in all the arts.

But Interlochen was expensive, prohibitively so. To her surprise, Jewel won a six-thousand dollar vocal scholarship, but this would cover less than three-quarters of the first year's tuition. Where she had been elated at having been accepted, Jewel became morose at seeing this opportunity elude her. But money was tight, and the remaining three thousand dollars might as well have been a million. Besides, once she paid the tuition there was the matter of her room and board. So, at the suggestion and with the efforts of her mother and her aunt Mossy, Jewel did what any showbiz kid in a similar situation would do: She put on a show. The benefit for Jewel's Interlochen tuition was held in Homer, and Jewel performed as the headliner. Initially uncertain whether such a benefit could sell enough tickets, Jewel's fears were allayed when the citizens of Homer showed up in droves. The place filled up and the audience, screaming and clapping, sent Jewel off to Michigan.

The Interlochen Arts Academy's approach was more formal than Jewel was accustomed to, but, then again, it had a prestigious reputation to uphold. Only a small fraction of applicants are granted admission, and this meant that many of her classmates had already undergone a great deal of formal training before they had even arrived. In 1991, for example, Interlochen was the only high school invited to perform at the Mozart Bicentennial Celebration at New York's Lincoln Center. Jewel would have her work cut out for her in order to prove she belonged with the other 430 students from around the world.

The faculty encouraged individual initiative, which suited Jewel perfectly. It was competitive, and there were ample opportunities for public presentation. Jewel was prepared to conquer the creaky old institution on her own terms, even if it took every ounce of her talent, skill, and endurance. Even at sixteen, Jewel wanted it all. She had a great deal to learn, however. "Classical [singing] was hard for me," Jewel has said. "I went [to Interlochen] thinking I'd get a scholarship for blues. They asked me to sing an aria and I didn't know what one was." She studied opera, which improved her vocal range and did wonders for her breathing. Doing repeated vocal exercises allowed her to control the timbre of her falsetto. She learned to look at singing from a purely technical standpoint, realizing that her voice was an instrument like any other.

Still, Jewel became frustrated by the rigidity of a purely classical training. Opera's complete lack of spontaneity was too scientific for her. What had once been so instinctual and intuitive for her was suddenly difficult and emotionless. Of course, this happens to any artist when they focus on technique, but it unnerved Jewel to be so isolated from inner expression. Yet she made the most of her experience at the school, studying dance, drama, and sculpture, as well as music. Everything she did at Interlochen she undertook with great enthusiasm. Voice instructor Ron Gentry has said that Jewel carried herself more like a teacher than a student. "She knew where she was going." Another voice instructor, Nicole Philibosian, noted that Jewel's self-confidence made her stand out, and that an abundance of talent was already apparent. "She was completely game to try anything," Philibosian said.

Trying anything also included trying to act. She set out to audition for the leading role of a dead woman who told tales from the grave in a play based on Edgar Lee Masters' *Spoon River Anthology*. Jewel felt thwarted, however, when she learned that voice majors weren't allowed to participate in dramatic endeavors. Jewel simply refused to accept this—after all, rules were meant to be broken. Not taking no for an answer, she continually pestered the drama department until they granted her an audition. They were humoring her, of course. No one without dramatic training could possibly expect to land a role against some of the country's best young actors and actresses.

Not only did Jewel land the role, she stole the show. And thanks to her stellar performance, Interlochen's policy was modified to allow nontheater majors to participate in the drama program. Jewel's willingness to experiment and to venture down untraveled artistic avenues was legendary during her Interlochen years. Yet, sometimes her eagerness was born out of necessity. To pay the bills, Jewel sang with a pianist in jazz clubs in and around Interlochen. She also was a figure model for an art class—fully clothed, that is. Jean Parsons, Interlochen's visual art division chair, remembers Jewel doggedly practicing guitar between poses. Over the course of endless classes, during the day, at night, and on weekends, Jewel did a fair share of composing new songs, Parsons recalled. "She has lived this thrifty, rather harsh life and built within her a strong constitution."

Jewel had already begun writing songs when she arrived at Interlochen. But—perhaps as a reaction to the restrictions of her classical training—songwriting ideas began to flood from her onto paper and four-track tape. While still a student, she made her first recordings, an eleven-song demo. Two of those songs, "Don't" (then called "Waltz") and "Dance Between Two Women," continue to be part of Jewel's current repertoire. "Dance" was inspired by an Interlochen yearbook photo of Jewel partnered with a fellow female student, which became the source of controversy on campus. The other songs remain unreleased—titles like "Billy," "Can't Have My Soul," and "Money." Jewel claims the inspiration to write those first songs came from watching people. "I find people fascinating," she said. "I think it's fascinating to see businessmen walking like cripples in their business suits, old women that giggle with their long gray hair. I love every fucked-up and beautiful thing about us." Sometimes love wasn't quite the inspiration for her early songs. One of them, written during her senior year, was composed out of disgust for the anorexic and bulimic dance students victimized by their boyfriends.

> *"Gonna walk down the street*
> *and seduce every man I meet*
> *because I'm having a bad day.*
> *I am not size six.*
> *My legs are not skinny as sticks*
> *and dammit, someone's got to pay . . ."*

For Jewel to really feel like a songwriter, she believed it was necessary to learn an instrument, so she picked up the guitar during her senior year. And she did it with seriousness and dedication. Aside from the natural beauty of the instrument, it helped her to investigate music from a completely different perspective. Not that she was a natural player by any means. In fact she has said that her dyslexia made it necessary for her to practice twenty times as hard as other guitarists. But learning the instrument would help to vary her compositions enormously, and it would reinvigorate her love of music. Most important, perhaps, the guitar would move Jewel down the road of self-sufficiency. With a guitar, Jewel knew, she was a one-woman band.

Her years at Interlochen were a turning point for Jewel, who learned to keep in check the freewheeling tendencies she had developed when performing with her father. Opera, which she had studied with great intensity, interested her little at this stage. It was enough for Jewel to learn that it takes a decade, maybe longer, for an opera singer to perform the great roles. Jewel was too eager to make music now. She had learned subtlety, timing, precision. The technique she acquired there—something she had resisted at first—would serve her well. The school brags that 95 percent of its graduates go on to the nation's "most distinguished colleges and conservatories," but it would prove to be the last formal training Jewel would seek.

Jewel wasn't interested in college. Instead, having visited her mom the previous summer—in San Diego, where she now lived—she headed west, guitar in hand, with only one question on her mind: What would she do with the rest of her life?

CHAPTER THREE

In the Rough

People shouldn't compromise their pride and health just to have roofs over their heads. And when you get to that point where you're willing to die for [something], nothing else matters. It's very hard to starve, you know?

It was 1992. Grunge was in full flower, and America couldn't get enough of the vulnerable gloom-and-doom coming from the mouths of Eddie Vedder and Kurt Cobain. People pulled out their flannels, and marketers celebrated the birth of a generation named X, a younger collection of would-be somebodys without particular aspirations.

Jewel watched the road whir past her as she traveled west by train. It occurred to her that she was growing up, and could no longer call herself a child. Soon enough, she would have to go out in the world and earn a living. Sure, she had worked all her life, singing with her father and the rest of the family, but this was different. Now Jewel would be responsible for herself. She had to make her own way.

Jewel had a piece of parchment that proved she had graduated from one of the finest arts institutes in the land. But as far as this eighteen-year-old was concerned, the diploma, plus fifty cents, as they say, couldn't even buy her a cup of coffee. She wasn't going to be an opera singer, nor was she interested in college. In fact, she was resentful of the prevailing notion that artists have to go to school to be considered artists. She wasn't interested in "running away," so seeing the world didn't necessarily appeal to her. What she really wanted, although she may not have known it yet, was for the world to see her.

Jewel's life now lay before her, a limitless, confusing jumble of possibilities. Yet she had taken a path throughout her life that clearly indicated that a career in music and performance was in the cards. It was a natural progression of her academic, professional, and personal experiences. But she wasn't so sure. She had had a good run, a grand musical education from the seedy barrooms in Alaska to the staid halls of academia at Interlochen, but what would she do next? Her muse had yet to tap her on the shoulder.

She'd already taken the first step by leaving Michigan. To help pay her way across the country, she cast aside classical vocal training in favor of good, old-fashioned busking, turning street corners into her stage and belting a few tunes for her supper. With guitar playing now among her list of artistic skills, she could at least feel self-sufficient. And much of the confusion she felt at this time went directly into her lyrics. Jewel has said, "In creativity, the easiest vein to access is pain. It consumes you, overwhelms you, and you have to write about it. But after a while it's a cop-out. You have to move on to the next phase, which is: 'Okay, what do I do about it?'"

Rather than experiencing the usual teenage wanderlust—

grabbing a backpack and exploring the U.S. or Europe—Jewel had the desire to travel inside herself. At eighteen, she was very aware of the need to continue on a spiritual journey. "I felt like there was a bird inside my chest that had become urgent inside of me, but I didn't really know which way south was, which way to fly, which way to migrate," Jewel said.

So the bird flew more or less in a southwesterly direction, spending some time in lovely Boulder, Colorado, in the foothills of the Rockies, until she finally landed in San Diego, city of sunshine and familiar faces. The laid-back town, she figured, would offer the perfect environment for her to figure out what to do with her life. And she would have the comfort of her family as she plotted her next move.

In many ways, Jewel's sudden postgraduate soul-searching was the most natural thing in the world. Like virtually all high school grads, the direction of her life to that point had been largely determined by education, where choice plays little part. Life would certainly be different if, as children, we were forced each September to find a job. School runs like clockwork, and it lulls us. Just when we get used to the rhythm of the school year, with its week-long breaks for Christmas and Easter, and luxurious reprieves during the summer months, reality rears its ugly head. And, suddenly, life can look very much like one long school year without vacations.

When Jewel arrived in southern California, she moved into a house with her mother and brother Atz in the inland suburb of Poway, about ten miles northeast of San Diego proper. Where coastal San Diego possesses arguably one of the most beautiful shorelines in all the world, Poway is just another suburb, like thousands of other suburbs across the country. A community situated between similar communities, dotted with endless rows of identical tract home complexes, L-shaped malls, fast-food joints, family restaurants, and extra-wide streets that all seem to have smooth new coats of tar. Here you'll find cavernous, warehouse-style super-duper stores like Costco, Price Club, Office Depot, Home Depot, Auto Parts Depot, ad nauseum.

For the Kilcher contingent, it was a far cry from the wilds of Homer where, if you wanted meat, you killed a cow. Even the comforts of suburban life were lost on them, offset by the high cost of rent and living expenses. It was a struggle for the trio, who were accustomed to living simply, on less. Soon enough, Jewel's brother flew the family coop and returned to Alaska.

For Jewel, reality was a formidable obstacle. She spent her first months in San Diego working a series of menial jobs in order to make the rent. "Icky jobs serving coffee and working in computer stores," Jewel remembered.

As a waitress, Jewel was skilled at eating and chatting with customers, but the art of actually "waiting" was something Jewel never quite managed to master. In the first place, it somehow irked Jewel that customers would "order" their food—that is to say, demand it. She had always been more comfortable with people who smiled and asked nicely for things, but Jewel soon found that people who were hungry often dispensed with pleasantries. Furthermore, Jewel was told, being a good waiter entailed never stopping moving. She was repeatedly reminded that she should never enter or exit a restaurant kitchen with empty hands. That during the slow periods there were many things to be done, including "marrying" ketchups or filling her salt and pepper shakers. Shaky tables could always be repaired during what Jewel considered down time, water glasses could be filled, desserts could be sold, and customers could be asked: "Is everything all right?"

No, Jewel had other ideas about restaurant work. Restaurants were places she could meet people of all ages and backgrounds.

She could observe human behavior, sadness, and joy, and she could earn an hourly wage and tips at the same time. She could schmooze with struggling musicians and she could scribble lyrics on the dupe pads that were provided for the purpose of taking customers' orders.

Another thing troubled Jewel about waiting tables. Her colleagues, who found her charming in spite of her tendency not to "overwork," often seemed stuck in their lives. Though many of them were artists and writers and musicians, Jewel got the sense that the restaurant world became too cushy for some people, causing them to lose sight of their long-term goals. Never would Jewel confuse the question of what she would be doing with her life with the question of what shifts she would be given.

Mother and daughter barely scraped by. Jewel recalls pooling the rent money together, bills in small denominations, and the last five dollars coming in tip-money quarters. Then, once the rent was paid, they still had to eat, but with what money? As a waitress, Jewel found herself scraping uneaten food off of customers' plates to keep from going hungry. She would even allow bosses to flirt with her and take her out to dinner. Jewel was fired from one job, she claims, because she refused to sleep with the boss.

She was flailing, "trying to hide," she has said. She tried to become friendly with rich people—which turned out to be spiritually taxing. As anyone might expect, these attempts led to dead ends. Luckily, Nedra was always there as a grounding influence in Jewel's confused life. "My mom would never let me get away from the fact that I had to figure out what my spirit wanted, that I did have a spirit and it did have a purpose."

Jewel got a good look at the backside of humanity while she punched the clock as a common laborer. Without money for the barest of necessities, life often became frustratingly ugly and desperate. Jewel developed a serious kidney infection, but without money to pay for the visit or the costly antibiotics, Nedra and her sick daughter were turned away from several clinics. Seeing her mother walk away, dejected, from all these medical facilities, was damaging to the teenager's spirit. "It just made you angry," Jewel said. "Nobody gave a shit. Nobody had to."

The gaping differences between the haves and have-nots became crystal clear to Jewel, who was getting tired of always licking at the fuzzy end of the lollipop. Before she turned her back on the nine-to-five world, she developed a fair share of resentment toward those who had money. "I used to really feel like it was an us against them kinda thing, especially being raised really poor," Jewel said. After getting the ax from one last waitressing job, Jewel figured there must be better, more interesting ways to be poor. After all, in the pursuit of survival, she felt like nothing so much as a hamster going nowhere on its Habitrail wheel. "If I could afford an apartment, I couldn't afford a car. If I could afford to pay rent, I couldn't afford food," she said.

Jewel was eighteen and going through a midlife crisis. She felt dirty compromising herself in order to maintain a roof over her head. She felt as though she were going nowhere fast, living perpetually in the past and the future, with no present to speak of. Finally, she had had enough. Her life felt passionless. "I thought, I've gotta figure this out. I have to look for purpose in my life." But what? Mere survival was sapping the life out of her. "Too much of our flesh is wasted on survival," she noted. "My hands and my creativity were going to waste . . . A lot of us just aren't taught that something you love can make you money."

Jewel discussed the situation with Nedra, who was working long hours at the time, teaching nutrition and self-improvement at a spa. Nedra was a great listener, a determined advocate of following one's dreams. In fact, mother was often more of a maverick than her daughter. Nedra always admonished Jewel to be brave and to trust herself. She encouraged her daughter to develop her thoughtful side, and to look at the world in many colors rather than merely in shades of black, white, and gray. She challenged Jewel, urging her, whenever possible, to spend five days alone in a cabin without contact from the outside world—or to go on body- and spirit-cleansing fasts. Jewel asked her mother a great number of questions: Should I do it? Should I throw myself into music? What about Dad's struggles? What if I fail? Should I have a plan B? Shouldn't I have a fallback plan? Nedra would reply: "If you have a fallback plan, you will fall back."

It was settled then. Jewel would sing. She would sing, she said, "until people never feel alone." She would indeed make her hobby her livelihood, much like her folksinging father, who'd taught her the ropes in those Alaskan hotels and bars all those years ago. Well, she thought, at least she wouldn't be singing in a musty old tavern, in some place where the life had been sucked from its pa-trons. Jewel had been writing music and was determined to de-velop material that would communicate her newfound feelings of hope, concern, and humanity. "All of a sudden her dream matched her needs," Nedra said. Jewel listened closely to her dreams and would soon communicate their power with others.

What did she have to lose? By this time mother and daugh-ter were so strapped for cash, Jewel was stealing toilet paper from fast-food restaurants. Finally it occurred to Jewel that being poor only had relevance or meaning if there was something attached to it. Now, at least, there was hope: Jewel was a musician.

During a late afternoon summer walk on Ocean Beach, Lou Niles, then a disc jockey at San Diego's modern rock station 91X, remembered a heart-to-heart he had with Jewel about art and life. Niles remembered her well, and liked her a great deal. He could see Jewel was in this for the love of it. He knew the first time he saw her jump onstage and sing that "she wasn't into the pinky-ring, long fingernails, and snorting cocaine type of career," Niles said. And though Jewel was ambitious, "She wasn't looking for the gold ring, just the brass one," he observed.

Preparing for lean times, at Nedra's suggestion mother and daughter bought two Volkswagen vans and moved out to the beach. The vans became their apartments, or, rather, condominiums: there was no more rent to pay. Jewel's was one of those round hippie microbuses from the late seventies, actually the last of the curvaceous collector's items Volkswagen made before introducing the boxy Vanagon. It was aqua blue, "in decent shape," according to Niles, with an off-white interior. The middle seat had been taken out, in favor of a "living room," and the back was modified by a friend so it could fit a bed.

If Jewel couldn't bum a shower from one of her Pacific Beach friends, her personal cleansing took place at a local restaurant bathroom or at Kmart. "They didn't bathe, and hardly ever shaved," Niles said. But it was clear Jewel was living this way for practical reasons, and not merely to espouse an alternative lifestyle. "She wasn't putting on airs. She wasn't trying to be a lost hippie chick in a van. But she did go around barefoot a lot." People took her seriously from the start. Jewel didn't drink or use drugs, and that earned her a lot of respect, even among those who did, said Niles. Of course, it didn't hurt that Jewel was a pretty young blonde. "If she were three hundred pounds and missing an arm, people wouldn't have checked her out so much," he said.

The liberation Jewel felt at living in her van and washing publicly was tempered only slightly by the cruel remarks and expressions of passersby, whose contempt for the homeless could barely be contained. As Jewel exited the Denny's at the busy intersection of Mission and Gabriel, where she had briskly washed her hair as best she could in the women's room sink, the masses on their way to work sneered at the young woman with soap still glistening on her wet blond mane. Yet the derision from the outside was a small price to pay. Jewel could just block it out. As in Homer, Jewel was living in a world isolated from almost everybody else. No, there weren't the huge expanses of land and space where she had lost herself as a child—instead she'd park her van near the water at Pacific Beach and let the misty scent of sea and sand waft into her small space. She'd fall asleep with the tranquil and inspiring soundtrack of waves crashing against waves.

Jewel had a favorite spot, next to a tree with blossoming flowers. Because curtains were hung and nobody could look into the windows, Jewel could pretend she was still in Alaska. The sunlight woke her softly in the morning, through the gauze of her homemade curtains, like a gentle alarm clock, or the hand of an angel. And the price, certainly, was right. Around this time she began to find inspiration in philosophy and art. She returned to Plato's *Symposium,* which she had studied in school, once again moved by its maxim that immortality can be achieved through love and beauty. "If we really put all of our passion into something, it will breathe, like a good sculpture, like a good Michelangelo, or Klimt," she said. "So what a beautiful thing to make your life your artwork . . . and to really pull in every experience." She read a lot at this time, often in the mellow glow of candlelight. Jewel soaked up the poetry of Pablo Neruda, and the inventiveness of Kurt Vonnegut's "Welcome to the Monkey House."

Waking up with the sun was something she cherished, along with gorgeous sunsets over the Pacific Ocean. And as the waves came crashing, they called to her. Surfing became first a curiosity, and then a spiritual rush for the young blonde. In appearance she seemed chiseled from the mold of the Beach Boys' "Surfer Girl," replete with a crooked nose, crooked teeth, and a happy smile.

Parking the van at night became something of a challenge—to drive along the coast in search of the gnarliest surf. One of her most memorable early surfing experiences came in Mexico with some surfer boys she'd met at a coffeehouse. "It was a pretty big day, five-foot overhead, rocky place, beautiful point," Jewel remembered. "A big wave came, I got inside, and looked at how big the waves were, got horrified, and I thought, what am I doing? I was kind of stupid, actually. I didn't know enough to be afraid."

But not knowing enough to be afraid was a blessing for Jewel. Had she journeyed to Los Angeles instead of San Diego, she may have encountered hundreds of singer/songwriters with the same dwindling hopes and dreams, looking for gigs and "shopping" their demos, each attempting to outdress, outsing, outplay, and outcool the rest. Working in restaurants or, if they're lucky, record stores. Luck was with Jewel. She was living on carrots and peanut butter, but at least she had hope. "You can't live with hopelessness," Jewel said. "[I realized] that for the rest of my life, I'm going to be okay. That's so amazing to get used to."

Free from financial constraints, she spent her time surfing, writing poetry, and hanging out in coffee shops writing songs. Her resentments began melting away. No longer did she have funny feelings toward the rich; instead she started to see the commonalities between people instead of the differences. Jewel started feeling compassion again. With compassion, she said, she no longer felt alone, even though her days were often solitary. "We all have fear of being without. We all want love. We all have passion. We all have aspirations no matter what end of the spectrum you are on, no matter what color you are."

Van life provided the freedom to observe, to meditate, and to create, to follow her life's passion. "We can't live without dreams, we are spiritual people, it's undeniable," she said. "We shouldn't spend our energy worrying about survival. We're creative human beings. We create cures for diseases, we create art, we move and change people, and we kill people."

Jewel spent her time looking at everything around her, and found inspiration in the strangest places. At a cafe she'd sip water while watching a couple making eyes or having a spat; she watched passersby look at their reflections in shop windows. She noticed how some people would wait until the traffic lights changed before they crossed the street—even if there were no cars in sight. She took solace in the way gulls circled the beach. She also paid close attention to her own inner life, with the knowledge that she should begin with what she knew of herself. "I grew up writing very autobiographically, dealing with my life through poems," said Jewel. "So when I started writing actual songs, they were accounts of life around me as I saw it."

She continued writing poetry during this time, and some of this work appears on the CD sleeve of her debut, *Pieces of You*. Her poem, "Upon Moving into My Van," offers a revealing glimpse of the freedom Jewel felt in her decision to jump off the working-class merry-go-round:

"I am what I always wanted to grow up and be
Things are becoming more of a dream with each waking day."

Around this time she composed one of her early songs, "Who Will Save Your Soul." She hadn't really written any songs since Interlochen, and she felt like composing something new to sing on the street during an adventure in Mexico. "I was just on a Greyhound bus ride and bored out of my skull with a pen in my hand." Truth be told, the inspiration for the song came from having met a man who, at nearly thirty years old, admitted that he'd never walked across grass with bare feet. It's just like Jewel's imagination to create an entire scenario about such a person, who takes for granted what she believed was an inalienable human right: to feel intensely the ground beneath her feet.

Soon, Jewel would feel a stage beneath her feet. When she worked at a Pacific Beach coffeehouse called Java Joe's, she met a singer/songwriter named Steve Poltz. A veteran of San Diego's grassroots music scene, Poltz had a regular gig at Java Joe's, thriving both as a solo artist and as the leader of the boisterous, crowd-pleasing band, the Rugburns. Jewel responded to his musical versatility immediately. Watching Poltz play—with only a voice, acoustic guitar, and a stool—opened Jewel's mind to the possibilities of that simple performance style. Once she had some material under her belt, she had only to watch Poltz very carefully, paying close attention to the way he connected with his audience. Soon she would be connecting with her own.

CHAPTER FOUR

Little Sister

* * ·
(·

We gotta start feeding our souls.

Jewel walked into the Innerchange Coffee House for the first time in early 1993, shortly after the place had opened. In the light of day it must have reminded her a bit of herself—it was all so new and seemingly out of place amid the comfortably worn atmosphere of Pacific Beach. It was like walking head-on into a piece of Indian jewelry—its motif was heavily turquoise, in honor of its address, 828 Turquoise Street. The gleaming tables were encircled by new, sturdy wooden chairs and set with unchipped crockery and shining silverware. Fixtures sparkled, and even the cork-bottomed bar trays were unstained, stacked neatly next to the register. But something was missing: this little cafe needed to be broken in, much like the young singer/songwriter.

And so it was, as the Innerchange quickly became a place to escape for San Diegans—on weekends especially—when masses from nearby suburban hamlets like Escondido, Poway, and Rancho Bernardo flocked to Pacific Beach's cafes and shops. Of all the local coastal communities, Pacific Beach was the most welcoming. The lazy beach town lacked the ritzy trappings of La Jolla, with its unattainable air of opulence, immaculately maintained galleries, and pricey boutiques. But it was more inviting than the broken-down bohemia of Ocean Beach to the south. Pacific Beach was a friendly patch of seaside heaven at the north end of Mission Bay—funky and relaxed enough for hipsters, with a charm that attracted the upper crust, where greasy food stands, surf shops, and sandy sidewalks coexist peacefully with the Häagen-Dazs shop and Banana Republic. The main drag, two blocks from the Pacific, attracted a salty mix of surfers, military brats from the base at nearby Oceanside, frat boys from San Diego State. At night, the strip teemed with slow-moving crowds and rows of old American cars. The evening crowds often stopped in at the Innerchange for a double cappuccino or a fresh-baked raisin scone.

Outside the coffeehouse, Jewel would have been difficult to spot among the crowds. She was just one of dozens of blond surfer girls whose golden hair turned ever paler with the summer months' exposure to a lazy coastal sun. Clad in baggies and a T-shirt, often barefoot with grains of sand between her toes, Jewel spent a fair amount of time parading around Pacific Beach, dreaming in the daylight. At night, she strolled the neighborhood alone in tattered jeans, slinky, spaghetti-strapped tops, and flip-flops. Once inside the Innerchange, her Thursday night haunt, she brightened, dressing in thrift-store finery or a dress made by a friend. When she took to the stage to sing, it was as though a light were inside her.

Soon after arriving in Pacific Beach, Jewel was drawn to nighttimes at the Innerchange, and to the magical convergence of artists and musicians that swirled around it. This java joint would become her Paris—she said it was every bit as inspirational and literary as the haunts of Hemingway, Fitzgerald, and Gertrude Stein, and their generation lost in the twenties. Over the two years Jewel resided in Pacific Beach and in the company of its musicians, she became their Fitzgerald, the outsider, the lovely, complicated charm in their circle. Together, the young musicians would talk about music, as expected, but also philosophy, politics, poetry, and Nabokov, Nabokov, Nabokov. They were pillars of support for each other. "We were all starving," Jewel recalled, "but here are all these talented, brilliant writers—I just felt so honored to be around them and writing with them."

Jewel had few friends when she first arrived in San Diego, and she felt isolated and alone but for her mother's company. It was a blessing of sorts, lending her the time alone on the beach to make music. Like any writer, Jewel began alone with the blank page. With guitar in hand, Jewel could create myriad creative combinations. Like every guitar, it had six strings and twenty frets, 120 notes, thousands of chords, millions of harmonic and melodic possibilities. Even a simple D major, she learned, could be played a dozen ways. As she struggled to craft her early songs, the pages on her dog-eared spiral pad became less legible and more tattered in the back pocket of her faded Levi's.

She began with poems. She had been writing them since the age of six, when her mother conducted poetry workshops for her and her two brothers in their Homer, Alaska, home. Jewel's poems were little gusts of words, often introspective and revealing, simple but deceptively profound observations of herself and the world around her.

However, she learned soon enough that poems could not always be recast as songs. At heart she was a wordsmith, far better at writing a turn of phrase than completing a melody. "I get very insecure about it all," Jewel has said. "I'm much more loyal to my poetry . . . with words I'm much more confident." In composing music to her words, there was structure for her to consider. Does this song have a chorus? A break? A bridge? Is there a clarity and progression to the verses? And what about honesty? She strove from the first to make music that was both intensely personal and universally truthful. She had recently read Gertrude Stein's *The Making of Americans* and had been struck by the passage, "I am writing for myself and strangers . . . everybody is like someone else to me . . . so I write for myself and strangers."

Naturally, she chose simple melodies that could accommodate her lyric-based style, but her hands weren't primed for playing the guitar at length, as she had been playing for less than a year. So she set about building calluses. At first, her fingertips turned so raw that after only minutes of playing she'd need to stop. She'd have to start again, like every guitar player before her: acquiring blisters for her blisters. Building calluses.

She was faced with every guitar player's paradox: relieving the pain by playing through it. "My hands are young when it comes to the guitar, and they can't do what my head hears." As if that were not enough, Jewel found that, because she had not yet learned to modulate and build a song's dynamics, she had a tendency to speed up as she moved into the body of a tune. And the lazy, sexy drive of her songs lost their power when played too quickly.

But the problems went deeper as Jewel transformed from an amateur poet into a professional musician. She had difficulty when she tried to sing and play guitar simultaneously. She was confused about writing, playing, and singing. Suddenly there was too much to consider for a young musician so new to her trade.

The solitude of living at the beach helped Jewel get more comfortable with songwriting. She watched other musicians whenever she could, learned from their performances, writing styles, and their influences. She was surrounded by veterans and newcomers, all of whom were busily creating new material.

Jewel found inspiration in the talent of those around her, realizing immediately that much could be learned—everything could be learned—from these people. She saw herself at the beginning of a bright career. Recognition, she realized, meant having faith and, more than anything else, working hard, perfecting the skills of her trade—playing, singing, performing, but most of all, writing. "Instead of focusing on what I didn't have," she said, "I would focus on what I wanted."

At the time, the national music media was sending signals that the San Diego music scene was poised to become the next Seattle. Unlike the self-destructive drone that enveloped Seattle's grunge scene, from the backstreets of San Diego came the lewd, crude, satirical sounds of Mojo Nixon. His "Elvis Is Everywhere" and "Debbie Gibson Is Pregnant with My Two-Headed Love Child" had both been MTV hits in the mideighties, laying the groundwork for the don't-take-anything-too-seriously attitude that characterized the early nineties in San Diego. Country Dick Montana's Beat Farmers were the boozy spiritual heirs to Nixon, and the Rugburns also teetered on the lunatic fringe. "San Diego was really happening in ninety-three, ninety-four, half of ninety-five," said former 91X disc jockey Lou Niles. More clubs than ever were geared toward live music. There were only a handful of singer/songwriters in town. Jewel's competition in San Diego's folksy coffeehouse circuit included traditional singer/songwriters like Joy Eden Harrison, Byron Nash, Gregory Page, and Steve Harris.

The high-octane shockabilly of Rocket from the Crypt also helped put San Diego on the musical map at this time, making some noise in the national arena. These bands filled clubs, like the Casbah in the revitalized Gaslamp Quarter and the Iguana just across the border in Tijuana, with sweaty, good-natured rock 'n' roll. No one was thinking about getting rich from music—the stakes were low and the musicians were in it for a laugh and a beer.

Steve Poltz, frontman of the Rugburns, was a sandy-haired hipster ten years Jewel's senior, whose wisps of facial hair brought friendly comparisons to Shaggy from the old *Scooby Doo* cartoon series. He would describe his band, with more than a hint of irony, as "really slow speed-metal"; their first record was titled *Morning Wood*. Rugburns stage shows were manic, chaotic affairs, yet still they could slow it down to a tender ballad. The band was enormously clever, their lyrics intelligent and humorous, their following loyal and vocal. Jewel quickly became a fan, mesmerized by Poltz's versatility and knack for crafting a song. In tunes like "Silver Lining," he could be bitingly witty and disarmingly heartfelt in a single verse:

> *"I turn on my TV*
> *They got the talking heads in space*
> *It used to be so easy*
> *to have a little faith."*

Jewel met Poltz while working at a coffee shop called Java Joe's, where Poltz had a regular gig. Jewel said, "I told him I sang, and he got me up there one night, to humor me, I think." In truth, he was teaching her an important lesson: that more than anything else, singers sing—and songwriters write.

They grew closer after that night, and Jewel began an intimate relationship with Poltz, who taught her not only about music, but also about surfing. Gradually they became lovers, confidants, and traveling companions. In Jewel, Poltz saw a fiery young beauty whose determination, he thought at the time, exceeded her talent.

For her part, Jewel was an eager student who found in Poltz a mentor. From him she sought advice and ideas, soaking up the knowledge he had gleaned from nearly a decade on the San Diego music scene.

They soon began collaborating on material, as Poltz exposed Jewel to the concept the verse/chorus/verse structure and also helped her bring humor into her then-deadly-serious writing. Jewel, in turn, appeared in the Rugburns' video "Hitchhiker Joe," from the band's *Morning Wood* album.

Hitching south of the border, leaving behind the often tepid California waves in search of the righteous surf became a habit for the pair. With just their thumbs and boards, they relied on the kindness of strangers to carry them past Escondido down to Rosarito Beach or, if they were lucky, farther down the coast to Ensenada, where they could feast on ten-dollar plates of lobster and refried beans.

The couple had a tendency to attract excitement. On one summertime excursion, Jewel approached a band of Federales armed with automatic weapons, and asked where she and Poltz might find a boat to look at whales in the ocean. The Federales said they could ride in their boat. Once they were out in the bay, Jewel asked the Feds what they were looking for. She quickly found out: Her hosts spotted a boat full of drug smugglers near the shore and promptly raced back to land. Before she knew it, the Federales and smugglers had squared off in a gun battle. The singing/songwriting couple were soon facedown on the dirt, caught in the crossfire. Most of the time, though, the couple's Mexican trips were like extended honeymoons, filled with inspired moments of creativity and passion. Together, Poltz and Jewel wrote the tender love ballad "You Were Meant for Me" on one of these south-of-the-border escapes, putting what they felt for each other into words and music:

> *"I know you love me*
> *And soon you will see*
> *You were meant for me."*

Back on the San Diego scene, Jewel studied the way the Rugburns played to the crowds, and how their shows developed a momentum in the same manner as a song, building slowly to a satisfying denouement. The band's performances were more than shows, they were events, and one was never like another. Jewel did not want to imitate them—after all, Poltz often performed in a prom dress, without underwear. Jewel was less interested in those kinds of novelties, but she realized the need for diverse, entertaining performances that weren't simply live—but alive. She asked Poltz not how she could get a gig, but rather how she might develop a following as loyal as the Rugburns' audiences. Poltz's advice in return was that she find a regular gig. He told her to play in the same place on the same night each week and, next thing you know, he quipped, the limousines will be coming through town. He was joking, of course; but Jewel apparently took him seriously. Even at eighteen, she had an eye on the bottom line: If she was going to perform, she was going to succeed at it.

Jewel's interest in performing grew, and Poltz continued to champion her. He decided to introduce her to Nancy Porter, the owner of the Innerchange. There, on a weekday afternoon, as the lunch people were leaving and before the evening staff had yet arrived, Jewel sat at one of the tables and played Porter two folksy, lilting numbers. The second song she performed was a remarkably self-assured version of "Who Will Save Your Soul."

Nancy Porter was impressed. "At the time she was really rough," Porter remembers, "[but] she had the talent. She disciplined herself and kept at it. I knew she'd succeed." Before Jewel's performance that afternoon, she had simply been Steve's girlfriend. But that day Porter saw in Jewel something remarkably genuine: her songs were like short stories, inspirational and uplifting, and totally unlike the irony-laden tunes of most San Diego bands. Would this surfer girl fit in? It didn't matter, Porter thought. Jewel was a diamond in the rough. So she was given a coveted slot at the Innerchange: Thursday nights.

The day before her first evening performance, Jewel stood around the block from the Innerchange for much of the afternoon, chasing down all comers with the announcement of her gala debut. It was one of those exceptionally hot days where the air is so thick you can see it bounce from the street in dizzying waves, the kind of day where passersby just want to get where they're going without being bothered. Nevertheless, Jewel attempted to hand out flyers on the streets of Pacific Beach—to surfers, Rastafarians, and to preteens just off the bus from the burbs, headed for the beach to catch a few rays. Most people walked right by her outstretched arm, refusing the flyer, ignoring her. Some guys promised to show up only if they could get a date with her. By sunset, Jewel was flustered and frustrated, with nearly as many fliers in hand as when she had begun.

The following night, the sight of the Innerchange filled with empty tables and lonely chairs was more than Jewel could handle. Staff outnumbered clientele. Right before her set, she stepped outside to search for her composure, wondering if singing to a nearly empty house was worth it. Then she thought about her father. Atz would have told her, "Darlin', the show must go on. If you can't perform for the crowd, perform for yourself." So she went back inside, and personally welcomed the handful of spectators before hitting the stage and singing her songs for the first time in public.

Jewel learned an important lesson that night: Pay attention to the nuances of your crowd. Rather than pretending the place was packed, she endlessly thanked the attendees for coming, and for staying. All those years singing with her father in Alaskan dives and performing alone in Michigan piano bars had trained her for handling such a small audience and dealing with the hard times. As her set progressed, her confidence grew. And, in a way, having such a small crowd was a blessing in disguise. She could experiment.

The cult of Jewel has grown to such an extent that thousands now claim to have seen the young songbird on that first Thursday-night in early 1993. In truth, there were seven people in the Innerchange, and one of them was onstage. At three dollars per head, Jewel had only eighteen dollars to show for her performance that night, and it was obvious to her that the Thursday-night gig was not likely to be lucrative—for the short-term anyway. But she kept returning to what her mother told her when they'd decided to move into their vans: Be brave and listen to yourself. And despite the hardship, Jewel had never felt more free. Her dietary staples at the time were peanut butter and carrots, and extra crackers from cups of soup. If she had an extra five bucks in her pocket, well, life was good.

"[The Innerchange] was looking for business. They said I could keep the door money, and they would keep the coffee sales," Jewel said. "And so I stuck with them and we both struggled together to get more people to come in."

She had always been satisfied or, rather, inspired by what most would call modest or impoverished circumstances. Performing a set through the whir and grind of a nearby cappuccino machine never deterred her; it made her stronger. In these early Innerchange gigs she managed to work through the technical difficulties any young performer faces—having to look down at her fretboard while she strummed those early songs, struggling to keep her mouth to the microphone so that her eloquent lyrics and angelic young voice could ring loud enough over the conversational hum of the coffeehouse.

And, slowly, she developed a reputation as the girl with the golden voice and the heart to match. People came to see her from week to week, and she felt compelled to give them new material. She wrote songs on drink napkins, on the backs of matchbooks, on the palm of her hand. Her lyrics spoke of her circumstances. Sometimes they were so close to home, they caught in her throat.

> *"The sun sets across the ocean*
> *I'm a thousand miles from anywhere*
> *And my pocketbook and my heart*
> *Both just got stolen."*

Poltz, for his part, introduced her to the popular music that had eluded her during a childhood in Alaska. Believing her to be a little bit of a cultural misfit, Poltz moved her past Ella Fitzgerald and Yma Sumac, playing her contemporary artists like the Replacements and Tom Waits. He introduced her to Joni Mitchell's *Blue,* which came as a revelation. Mitchell's introspective themes, tinged with wry humor, struck a chord with the young songwriter. When she heard lyrics to Mitchell songs like "All I Want"—"I am on a lonely road and I am traveling / Looking for the key to set me free"—Jewel felt like she had found a kindred spirit. And Mitchell's song "California" solidified Jewel's notion of a story-telling, conversational style:

> "Went to a party down a red dirt road
> There were lots of pretty people there
> Reading *Rolling Stone*
> Reading *Vogue*."

But Poltz had the biggest impact on her at the time. He worked with her songs, rearranging them, focusing them. "Steve's been a big influence," Jewel said. "He's as good as all the song-writers, as good as John Prine . . . [and] he never stops."

Jewel's Innerchange shows were rambling, freewheeling, emotion-packed affairs, often lasting more than three hours—a far cry from the tight, professional set she would play years later at the Lilith Fair. Poltz, Frank Drennen, John Katchur, and other musicians often joined her on stage for improvisational jams.

Once upon a time, while singing a particularly personal lyric, she'd had trouble looking her audience in the eye. Eventually she learned to take her songs right to the crowd, using them, chal-lenging them, and riding the emotional waves they sent up to her from their seats. She wasn't afraid to pause, or to play longer in-strumental breaks. She wasn't afraid to be soft—very, very soft. She developed a natural feel for dynamics—not only within a phrase or a song—but within the set as a whole.

Sometimes while introducing a song, she would speak off-the-cuff, telling a personal story, a humorous anecdote. She told long-winded tales. She could even turn her incessant guitar-tuning into amusing entertainment. She had a penchant for flar-ing her nostrils at hecklers, for stopping them with her stare, and also for laughing at her own jokes. On a whim, short songs would

Left: Jewel as she appeared on TNT's *The Wizard of Oz* in 1995.
Credit: Victor Malafronte/Archive Newsphotos

Right: By the time Jewel appeared at Hollywood's American Cinematheque Moving Picture Ball in 1996, the hippie folkstress had made the transformation to stylish chanteuse.
Credit: © Vincent Zuffante, Star File Photo

Right: Jewel took time out from recording in 1996 to provide a special concert in Woodstock for her fans, called Jewelstock.
Credit: Gregory E. Dunn

Left: Jewel reads her poetry at Jewelstock, 1996.
Credit: Gregory E. Dunn

Right: Jewel with her mother, Nedra Carroll, at the nomination ceremony for the Thirty-Ninth Annual Grammy Awards. Nedra has been a pillar of emotional and spiritual support during Jewel's ascent.
Credit: Stephen Tropp / Celebrity Photo Agency

Left: The dress that shocked the world: Jewel leaves little to the imagination at the 1997 Grammy Awards in New York.
Credit: © Vincent Zuffante, Star File Photo

Jewel sings the national anthem at the start of Super Bowl XXXII on
January 25, 1998, at San Diego's Qualcomm Stadium.
Credit: Reuters/Sam Mircovich/Archive Photos

The dream comes true: Jewel works the crowd during the taping of MTV Unplugged in 1997. Credit: MTV Networks (publicity photos)

Left: Jewel and her boyfriend, Michael, make a dashing couple as they make their way into the 1997 MTV Movie Awards in Santa Monica.
Credit: Gilbert Flores / Celebrity Photo Agency

Right: Jewel always makes time for her fans.
Credit: Gregory E. Dunn

Above: Jewel goes through the motions at the Hard Rock Casino in Las Vegas, New Year's Eve, 1998. Here she sings "Satellite" with the Red Hot Chili Pepper's Flea on bass.
Credit: Paul Kolsby

Right: Jewel rocks in the new year in Vegas.

February 1998: A stunning Jewel dressed to the nines for the
Fortieth Annual Grammy Awards in New York City.
Credit: Reuters/Mike Segar/Archive Photos

be extended into jams. She drank water from a jug, joking about the day a water company would offer her a corporate sponsorship: "Jewel, on tour. Brought to you by Evian!"

There was never a set list, and she often took requests. She played new songs she hardly knew, or made them up on the spot. She developed the necessary fearlessness that any talented musician must embrace. If someone got up to leave or go to the bathroom, Jewel would stop, midsong, clear her throat, and begin talking to the departing audience member. "Are you leaving?" she'd ask, then she'd turn to the audience and ask them to say good-bye. She learned to turn on a dime, use the crowd's energy to make them laugh, think, and listen. More and more people would come up afterwards to tell her how moved they'd been. The shy, reserved nature she felt elsewhere in life melted away before her audiences. She found her home on a stage, feeding off the love in strangers' stares.

And the audiences, the frat boys and surfers, fellow musicians and suburban couples, even the servicemen, held onto every note, brought their love and support, and pushed Jewel to even greater heights. Her message of hope had begun to have an effect on the crowds. Regulars became devotees, and audiences began to possess something like the devotional fervor of fans of the Grateful Dead. Bootleg tapes were made and circulated, and Jewel herself relied on them to help recapture nuances of songs she had just created. People traded particularly rocking versions of "Rocker Girl" or "Pieces of You" with impromptu lyrics that answered hecklers who admonished Jewel to "take it off." "Stupid boys," Jewel would sing in response, without missing a beat, as if it were a part of the song. She could appear vulnerable before an audience, and yet derive great power from that vulnerability: she was defiant, fearless, totally confident of the power of her music. "Opening your heart [doesn't] make you more vulnerable," Jewel said, "it protects you."

Over the course of her nine-month stint at the Innerchange, Jewel's Thursday night shows became a must-see in San Diego, and the Innerchange changed along with Jewel. In less than a year, the rickety wooden chairs had lost their balance. Tables wobbled, despite the help of matchbooks set under the legs. Their luster had been erased by too much intimate contact with hands and beer, worn sponges and abrasive detergents. The tiny stage, too, bore the scars of recent history. And the mike stand, from too much adjustment, had two positions: tall and short.

During these months, Jewel had become a centerpiece of the San Diego scene, garnering the respect of fellow musicians. No longer just Poltz's guitar-playing girlfriend, her rising prominence cast new light on their relationship: they were now the king and queen of the local music scene, and they were inseparable. After a life on the outside looking in, Jewel was suddenly at the center of a hurricane, her hurricane. And it was good. She was doing what she loved, surrounded by people she trusted.

Best of all, it seemed the more she immersed herself in her writing and performing, the less she thought about the "big break," which in so many cases can paralyze a performer, creating expectations, resentments, rivalries. As her mother had advised, she followed her heart. "I prayed every night in my van that my dream would come true," Jewel remembers. She worked hard because she enjoyed playing well and entertaining people; the only hunger she felt was to surpass herself artistically, and to learn everything she could from the other musicians in her circle. She loved to watch others playing music, any kind of music, as long as it was played with conviction. And she learned onstage that she could bring this same pleasure to her audience.

Yet, in the fervent reception of her performances, one thing could not be mistaken. She was standing out from the crowd of San Diego performers. An early rave came from the local rag *Slamm*, which wrote, "Her voice is many things, all of them beautiful. When she opens up, the sound is crystalline and pure."

And whether she sensed it herself, those around her knew something was coming around the corner. Jewel didn't know what it was, and she forced herself not to fantasize too much, but one chilly spring night in 1994, she showed up at the Innerchange a few minutes before her Thursday night gig and couldn't even get in. A line of people waited outside at the door, and she thought there was some kind of problem. She peered in the front window—and suddenly it dawned on her. It's a good thing the fire marshal was nowhere close because there wasn't an inch of Innerchange that wasn't packed with music lovers. When Jewel walked through the door, she bowed her head, somewhat embarrassed by all the attention. But there was a problem: How would she get to the stage? Someone suggested she climb from table to table. It was the only answer.

And there Jewel was, teetering slowly across the rickety tables scattered like lily pads, guitar draped across her back, until she assumed her position at the mike, where she waited to begin for a full three minutes until the applause died down.

CHAPTER FIVE

The Seduction

* * *

So often our dreams become our hobbies and it deadens our passions.

Buzz is something that can't be manufactured. It just happens, like an unstoppable force of nature. From an outsider's perspective it seems as though an artist toils in obscurity one minute, dreaming the impossible dream; and in the next she's the biggest star in the galaxy.

Lots of people get paid lots of money to try to create a buzz, which explains why record companies employ public relations staffs. But if the record labels had a magic formula for buzz, they would certainly keep it under lock and key. What the industry creates in its dogged pursuit of buzz is actually hype.

Real buzz begins with word of mouth. And Jewel's name was seemingly on the lips of everyone who came to see her at the Innerchange. Fans told their friends about the young singer; they in turn told their friends. The result was like a snowball rolling down a hill. When Thursdays at the Innerchange became a must-go, and Jewel became a must-see, eventually her name spread northward, to the sprawling metropolis of Los Angeles.

The San Diego music scene had already been anointed by the press to follow in the footsteps of two other American cities: Seattle, which brought us Soundgarden, Nirvana, and Pearl Jam; and Chicago, home of Smashing Pumpkins, Urge Overkill, Veruca Salt, and Liz Phair. The music media had been waiting impatiently for San Diego to explode with a Next Big Thing, but so far it hadn't obliged. Then, suddenly, the city presented Jewel Kilcher, an odd choice when you consider that the alternative rock underground was the city's core scene.

She may actually have been the last person in San Diego to comprehend the commotion that surrounded her. A record deal was the last thing on her mind. Like most people living in impoverished circumstances, Jewel was still thinking in survival terms, about where her next meal would come from. She wisely kept her distance from the buzz, concentrating instead on the work at hand. "All you can do is be honest," she said. But Jewel knew as long as she worked hard toward her goal, it would be okay to make mistakes. "I never thought I'd get a record deal. I never thought I'd make an album, or that my stuff would be good enough to [make one]."

So Jewel the singer/songwriter, like generations of musicians before her, became Jewel the grassroots entrepreneur. She sold a tape at her shows that she titled *Shiva Diva Doo Wop.* It featured "Painters," a version of which would later appear on *Pieces of You,* as well as live favorites that have yet to appear officially on record: "1,000 Miles Away," "She Cries," and "My Own Private God's Gift to Woman." An original drawing by Jewel was also included in the package. Posters—with artwork by Nedra—were also sold at shows. The image was a purple, glow-in-the-dark angel on a

blue background. Printed at the bottom were the words "Participate in Miracles." It was an appropriate message for Jewel's fans,
who were party to Jewel's miracle in progress.

Jewel was actually captured on record before she ever signed a
record deal. Her first official release was issued in early 1994 as
one of several San Diego artists to appear on a sampler called
Saint Doug, put out by station 91X, which was an early champion
of Jewel and other local bands like the Rugburns. Her contribution to the CD was a rendition of "Angel Needs a Ride," an ode to
hitchhiking and the lost souls who litter the highway, and one of
several Jewel songs that would include the word *angel* in its title.
Like much of her work, the tune was about a specific character,
but its lyrics resonated with Jewel's own journey to California
from Michigan, actual and spiritual:

> *"Her feet were worn and tired*
> *But as determined as a soul*
> *She left with no regrets*
> *But also no possessions did she own."*

A few months earlier, Jewel had struggled to fill the Innerchange, singing her songs for a nearly empty room. Next thing
she knew, people were peering in through windows steamed over
from too many breathing bodies inside. They were trying to get a
glimpse of the blond-haired wonder, playing her acoustic guitar,
breaking open her soul once a week, three hours at a time. Jewel's
fire burned bright; people wanted to be near the flame. And heat
always sells.

Her fans may even have been more excited by the label interest than Jewel was. "It was, like, you know, [I was] everybody's

daughter, everybody's sister." Innerchange owner Nancy Porter was so excited that she put up signs welcoming the labels to her establishment. The label people were overwhelmed by the fans' enthusiasm. The cult of Jewel was revving up.

Jewel hadn't yet learned that A&R (Artist and Repertoire) people, the record company talent scouts, had bottomless expense accounts; she hadn't learned the first rule of the starving artist: smile a lot and order the most expensive dish on the menu. Instead, she treated a Virgin A&R rep to a burrito. In exchange for the meal, the rep told Jewel she could make a record. Indeed, other A&R people told her the same thing, even without the burritos. Before long, the princes came a-courting. Jewel still lived in her van, as limos carrying fat-cat record industry execs began maneuvering through L.A. traffic, down the San Diego Freeway, past Camp Pendleton, past the nuclear plant at San Onofre, all the way down to the boho streets of Pacific Beach. Suddenly, Jewel's life began to take on a surreal quality. They'd wine and dine her, fly her to New York for showcases and fancy dinners, promise her the world. At midnight, however, it was back to her pumpkin—to the reality of her van, to carrots and peanut butter and candlelight.

As it occurred to Jewel that her life might soon change, other things began to occur to her, too. This was no joke. Nedra was at every business meeting Jewel attended. She cut an impressive figure—blond, effusive, big-boned like her daughter. "She was a hippie mom; she was spiritual, had her head together," said Lou Niles. "She looked like an art teacher from a high school."

Most impressive, though, was Nedra's business sense, according to Niles, who himself had offered to represent Jewel during that time. "They were both very cautious and attentive to every word said in those meetings. They asked questions." Jewel and Nedra recognized how important it was to make the right decisions. "They were very aware of liars and 'weasels,'" said Niles. Jewel, for her part, had acquired a fine business sense, also. "Jewel was always nice to people, very genuine. Always. And she remembered everybody's name."

During this period of courtship, Jewel and Nedra refused to make any snap decisions. Once the offers came in, they resisted anything that made them feel even slightly uneasy. The offer wasn't right. The executive was sleazy. They didn't understand her music. They were looking for the quick buck. But somehow Jewel and Nedra trusted the spirits to guide them. And then, the spirits—as they had done for Jewel again and again—delivered. One fateful Thursday night in early 1994, a savvy Russian immigrant named Inga Vainshtein, a former movie executive, and manager of the San Diego band Rust, grabbed Jenny Price—then an A&R girl from Atlantic Records—and brought her down from Los Angeles to the Innerchange. Vainshtein had been tipped off about Jewel by John Hogan, Rust's lead singer. Hogan had been so impressed by Jewel's talents that Vainshtein acted quickly. Both women were hooked.

"What I noticed, aside from an incredibly talented woman," said Price, a petite, red-haired, twenty-eight-year-old dynamo, "was how completely silent the crowd was when Jewel sang." Price couldn't wait to get back to Los Angeles. The next morning, first thing, she called her boss—Atlantic Records president Danny Goldberg. "Forget the other artists [we've talked about]," she told him, "this girl is a poet." But this was perhaps too much enthusiasm for Goldberg at this hour of the morning.

"So do a demo deal with her," Goldberg replied.

"Forget the demo deal," Price countered. "We don't need a demo deal."

"Why?" Goldberg wanted to know.

Jenny Price was sure of herself. She wanted to say, "Because I just know." But going so far out on a limb, as she was about to do with Jewel, had its liabilities. Danny Goldberg was a noted civil libertarian and guru of bands like Nirvana. As his A&R person, Price was paid for her taste, and her ability not only to recognize talent, but to recognize the type of talent that can fill stadiums. At the time, Price was highly regarded, but young. She couldn't afford a major misfire—her status, her reliability, and the quality of her taste would suddenly be held in question. Such is the price to be paid for bottomless expense accounts. Price held on to the phone until her knuckles were white.

"Please, Danny?"

Goldberg finally relented. "Have her come in with her guitar."

A couple days later, the conference room at the Los Angeles office of Atlantic Records was reserved for the most important concert of Jewel's life. The audience would number only four: Danny Goldberg, Jenny Price, Kevin Williamson, and Nedra. Jewel called Price in the morning to confirm their appointment, explaining that she'd be driving up with her mother. Goldberg, for his part, left more than an hour free to spend with the young chanteuse. The clock ticked up to the appointed hour, and Jewel was a little late. The clock continued to tick—now Jewel was forty-five minutes late. Goldberg checked his watch, shook his head, and explained that his daughter was in town, that he had an appointment with her.

He told Price, "Even if she walked in the door right now, I wouldn't be able to . . ."

"Please don't go," Price pleaded.

Twenty minutes later, the inevitable happened: Danny Goldberg packed up his briefcase.

69

"Please wait, Danny? A little? Two minutes?" Goldberg checked his watch again and sighed. Fifteen minutes later he was riding down in the elevator.

Meanwhile, Jewel Kilcher and her mother were trying to figure out where the San Diego Freeway intersects with the Hollywood Freeway—or was it the Santa Monica Freeway? And is Freeway 101 the Hollywood freeway, or is that 110? Traffic was bad, which didn't help matters. Jewel must have been feeling frustrated in her blue VW bus, Nedra shaking her head, mother and daughter consulting their watches.

They arrived at the Atlantic offices two hours late, and Jewel played for all the aforementioned parties except the one she'd expected to meet—the decision-maker, record company president Goldberg. She would play, among others, what she thought her best calling-card song at the time, "Painters." Price sat in her high-backed chair and watched, somewhat distracted, still thinking about the fact that Goldberg hadn't been able to stay. Jewel, who had been trained to give a good performance "no matter what," must have tried very hard not to appear distraught.

On the spot, Jenny offered Jewel a demo, no strings attached. This meant that, at Atlantic's expense, Jewel would record some of her songs so that Goldberg could have a listen, but she would be in no way committed to Atlantic. Jewel was whisked to Cherokee Studios in Hollywood where, with the Robb brothers—producers of the Lemonheads' 1992 pop gem, "It's a Shame About Ray"—she recorded some thirty songs. After a quick mix, the demo was hand-carried to Danny Goldberg.

It took every bit of resolve for Jenny Price to resist the urge to stand directly over Goldberg's shoulder while he listened to the demo. And when he did, his answer was: "It's all right."

"All right?" Price asked.

"Yeah."

Price shook her head. This was not the response she was looking for. Far from it. But here is where she proved her worth. A less confident A&R person would've conceded defeat. If Price had simply said, "You're right, she's just all right," she might have gotten out of a jam without too much damage having been done, save for the cost of the demo. Instead, though, Price stuck to her guns. She wrangled, she prodded. She refused to budge. And Danny Goldberg trusted her enough to find himself at the Innerchange Cafe in San Diego to see Jewel play the following Thursday night.

The next day, Friday, Price tried to keep her mind off Jewel, and on the rest of the day's business. She would not approach her boss, she would let him approach her. She would think about her weekend. She would let her mind wander. Perhaps she would even try to meditate. But it was no use. She spent the whole day wondering what Goldberg thought, and sometimes she would listen to Jewel's demo in her office, volume turned low. Lunchtime came and went, along with Price's spirits.

Here was the most talented new performer Price had perhaps ever seen, and she would fall through Atlantic's cracks. Price may have thought her own career was in jeopardy. After all, maybe she wasn't the best judge of talent. Maybe she was off here—way off.

At three o'clock on Friday afternoon, when other executives were tying up the week's business, or on the phone with friends making dinner plans for Saturday, Price looked out her office window to Sunset Boulevard below, where the grit of West Hollywood made way for the tree-lined opulence of Beverly Hills. Los Angeles could be a gloomy city, in spite of a sun that shone so relentlessly. By the day's end, the gloom had crept into her bones. Maybe she would crawl into bed and spend the weekend there.

Then the call came. Goldberg wondered if Price were around the office. Where else would she be? As she moved through the

Atlantic hallways to his office, heart skipping with every step, she imagined how he would deliver the bad news. Would he be angry for having driven one hundred miles in each direction, only to confirm that Jewel was just "all right"? Did he think she was terrible? Would he question Price's taste? Or question her "understanding" of just what sort of talent Atlantic Records strove to attract? As Price walked into her boss's office, it hit her. Would she get fired?

Goldberg looked up. "You were absolutely right," he said, "she's a career artist."

Price let the words sink in. Career artist. This meant she had not only been right about Jewel—that she was talented and could probably be a profit-maker for the label—but that Jewel would perhaps be the kind of talent even a successful A&R person encounters only a few times in a career. Jenny Price heaved a sigh of relief: She would celebrate this weekend.

Actually, Jewel did well by arriving two hours late and missing her initial meeting with Goldberg. Jewel's performance in the conference room may not have impressed him as much as the Innerchange show in front of a hundred adoring fans, dead quiet and crammed into a four hundred-square-foot room. And if Goldberg had been lukewarm, as he originally was, Jewel would never have put thirty songs to tape, at Atlantic's expense, with producers as gifted as the Robb brothers. Jewel might have signed with a lesser label and put out a lesser album, which might have been allowed to die without the proper support. Perhaps most important, however, is that the extra time allowed Inga Vainshtein room to operate. Inga, declaring Jewel a cross between Barbra Streisand (was it the nose?) and Meryl Streep, quickly befriended Jewel and Nedra and, along with Nedra, became her manager. Inga took the demo Jewel made—the one with no strings attached—and circulated it to other labels, most notably Virgin.

Consequently, there was other very serious interest by the time Goldberg saw Jewel at the Innerchange.

Vainshtein nudged Jewel toward Atlantic Records, which eventually needed little convincing. She signed a multialbum deal with the label. Jewel loved Goldberg's genuineness, calling him on the liner notes to *Pieces of You,* "the most soulful daddy-o in the music business."

To celebrate, Jewel and her mom moved out of their vans into a one-bedroom flat. Jewel also bought a used Volvo wagon and a beautiful new guitar—at a discount because it had an imperfection in its finish. Acknowledging Jewel's "star" status, Nancy Porter raised the admission price at the Innerchange on Thursday nights to a whopping $5. Even at that unheard-of price, it was easily the best entertainment bargain in San Diego. For your five bucks, you got a three-hour set of mostly original material. And Jewel rarely played the same set twice.

Instead, Jewel used her Thursday shows at the Innerchange as a laboratory for new material. These game-for-anything audiences helped Jewel return to her roots, and Thursday nights at the Innerchange reminded her more and more of the seat-of-the-pants performances she'd given with Atz a decade earlier. With one exception: Now, rather than playing to drunk, amputee veterans of foreign wars, Jewel had a slavishly devoted audience that held onto every lyric, every syllable. "I listened to the tapes [of these Innerchange shows] and I wasn't good . . . but I was really sincere. And that's what people really wanted."

Jewel's spontaneity before and during this period, and her willingness to write songs moments before she went onstage and try them out immediately, paid great dividends. She listened to these performance tapes and was a bit shocked: By the time she was ready to record *Pieces of You*, she had hundreds of songs from which to choose. But the last Innerchange shows were not merely spontaneous or productive. They became scenes of joyous celebration. On any of these Thursday nights one could expect a veritable hootenanny on stage, as the cream of San Diego's acoustic scene gathered at the gigs to jam with Jewel. Poltz was usually there; Rugburns Rob Driscoll and Gregory Page, Joy Eden Harrison, and Cindy Lee Berryhill also dropped by for a few tunes. Audiences were treated not only to songs, but to reminiscences and toasts to the magic of dreams. And if there was a sense of urgency on the crowded stage, it was because this magic that Jewel had brought to San Diego could not and would not last. Like Alice in Wonderland having to crouch lower and lower in a room the size of a matchbox, Jewel would soon outgrow these modest digs.

By declaring Jewel a career artist, Atlantic realized that Jewel's first album would serve as a taste of future possibilities. Multiplatinum sales were out of the question, they believed. Instead, the label was thinking about the long term, about baby steps. If Jewel sold a solid forty thousand units of her debut, she would have enough presence on radio to support a more ambitious second album. Atlantic execs could then pat themselves on the back for a job well done, plan a more accelerated marketing push, and then send her into the studio for album number two. Besides, singer/songwriters were not exactly tearing up the charts in 1994. It was a schizophrenic time for radio and MTV: spending time at number one were Nirvana's unplugged swan song, Snoop Doggie Dog's gangsta rap, and the homogeneous country pop of Garth

Brooks and Tim McGraw. It was a diverse group, but you wouldn't find any folksingers among them.

The label was merely being realistic, opting for a low-key intro where they could build Jewel slowly and organically, capturing the singer in the same element where she had become successful. "I can do a more serious polished album next time," Jewel said. "I want this one to be a look at my world and what I'm doing now, and I want to capture the rawness of it." As Price once said, "We wanted to capture a moment in time."

To that end, it was determined that Jewel should record at least a portion of what would become *Pieces of You* at the Innerchange, the very place where Jewel began as a solo artist, and where she found her voice. There would be plenty of time for Jewel to grow into a slick studio setting.

Meanwhile, Goldberg and Price set about helping Jewel find the appropriate producer. "My first concern was how I would exist in the business and remain true," Jewel said. "I was looking for a producer who wouldn't produce me. I had met with a lot of them, and they all wanted to take me to the potential of what I could be in a couple of years naturally. I was looking for somebody who would at least let me be who I was, so I could be honest and recognizable to myself and my fans. I went with Ben Keith for those reasons." Keith also had an impressive instrumental performance pedigree—he had played pedal steel guitar on Neil Young's *Harvest* and *Harvest Moon*, as well as on Patsy Cline's classic *I Fall to Pieces*.

Keith and Price paid close attention as a sound crew set up its equipment at Innerchange in San Diego in the summer of 1994. On July 28 and 29, four three-hour sets were recorded. And though Atlantic talked to Jewel about what she would play and what tracks would be strongest for the record, according to Price, "She plays whatever she feels like playing." The only thing certain was that "Who Will Save Your Soul" would be the record's centerpiece, the song that would introduce Jewel to the world.

Tickets cost $8 for those Innerchange shows, and to get one you had to be either very well connected, very rich in order to buy a ticket from a scalper, or willing to stay up all night waiting in line. Some at Atlantic were concerned that the presence of recording equipment would throw Jewel off. After all, these were no ordinary shows. Live albums are usually the domain of established artists working for record labels milking them for every conceivable penny, but this was Jewel's debut. She had nine hours of tape to hit her emotional mark, play flawless guitar, and be at the peak of her voice.

So, although Atlantic wanted to present Jewel to the world as a singer/songwriter, the label still hedged its bets. Jewel was dispatched to the studio to record additional tracks for *Pieces of You*. Perhaps she was initially hesitant about the studio environment, but this was not just any studio. It didn't hurt that she would record "Who Will Save Your Soul" and "You Were Meant for Me" at Redwood Digital, located at Neil Young's Broken Arrow Ranch in northern California. It also didn't hurt Jewel that she was accompanied by Young's friends The Stray Gators. Needless to say, Jewel became an eager student. She was probably more than a little overwhelmed, soaking up the musical war stories told by the legendary veteran musicians—Spooner Oldham on keyboards, Robbie Buchanon on piano, Tim Drummond on bass, and Oscar Butterworth on drums. Jewel also had assistance from the ex–Go Go's guitarist Charlotte Caffey, who helped Jewel with arrangements on "Pieces of You," "Foolish Games," and "Near You Always."

Perhaps best of all, Jewel got to play Hank Williams' old Martin guitar on "Don't." She could hardly believe it. "I just sat there and tried to vibe in the energy," she said. Before too long, everyone was. The old-timers were soon comparing Jewel to Janis Joplin.

_[*]

In the wake of the record's release, Jewel played two sold-out, emotional shows at San Diego's Hahn Cosmopolitan. It was a farewell of sorts, a graduation party for the valedictorian going off to face the world. The crowd was filled with familiar faces, Innerchange regulars who had seen Jewel transform from a shaky caterpillar into a confident, beautiful butterfly. The show began with material from *Pieces of You*, before Jewel dug into her illustrious bag of tricks, treating this special audience to unreleased material like "Perfectly Clean," "Swedish Lullaby," and "501 Beauty Queen." Steve Poltz hopped on stage for a rousing rendition of "Silver Lining," followed by the rest of the Rugburns, who rocked through a quartet of songs. The highlight was a revved-up version of "My Own Private God's Gift to Woman." For the encore, Jewel took the stage alone, awash in light. She gave quiet, heartful renditions of "Angel Standing By" and "Amen."

Before she left the stage, she gave a commencement address to her San Diego fans: "My fellow music lovers . . . I was just a girl who was tired of waitressing, and people believed in me and fed me by coming to my shows. Without my friends in San Diego . . . I would still be hungry in my van . . . Sometimes record labels think they sell albums—but they don't—they help, but it's you guys who help me. So often our dreams become our hobbies and it deadens our passions. I love my life and want to thank you all. I know our lives are separate and that none of you have to care about my happiness, but that you do things like taking the time to call radio stations means a lot to me. I hope I can give back as much as I'm given . . ."

Pieces of You was released on the last day of February 1995, very much the creation of a woman just beginning to understand her potential and her art. The record's initial sales were appalling—much lower even than Atlantic's modest expectations. In fact, so few copies were sold that Jewel may have even considered reapplying for one of those waitressing jobs.

CHAPTER SIX

Soul for Sale

I'm funny that way—I always worry and then everything goes okay and then I worry again.

Even before the official release of *Pieces of You*, Jewel was already doing road work. Atlantic's marketing honchos decided that Jewel should play acoustic shows without a band—just a girl with her guitar and her big voice—thereby reinforcing the simplicity of the music on her record. Their plan was to duplicate in other cities what she had done in San Diego, to mimic the Innerchange's atmosphere by booking her in coffee shops around the country. She would stay on the road for the better part of three years. After all, America was a huge country; there were many other San Diegos to conquer.

Jewel was a professional singer/songwriter now, recording for the same label as Aretha Franklin and Led Zeppelin. Obviously, she would perform a schedule far less relaxed than once a week at the Innerchange. So Atlantic cooked up an ingenious but grueling proposition: For four weeks, on more or less consecutive days, Jewel would play the same rotation of four coffee shops in four different cities, usually college towns, before moving on to an entirely different set of cities. It was the kamikaze, grassroots, and inexpensive way to build a fan base. "I never expected to sell a lot of albums," Jewel has said. "If I wanted to have a long-term career like Neil Young, it would just take touring."

She played, for example, Washington, D.C., Philadelphia, New York, then Cambridge, Massachusetts—bopping from one city to another in an Econoline van with only a tour manager for company. In fact, on February 28, 1995—the day *Pieces of You* was released—Jewel celebrated with a performance at New York's Ludlow Street Cafe. *Celebrated* may not be the appropriate word, however: the following day she rode for five hours up Interstate 95, through New Haven and Providence, on her way to Boston and her show in Cambridge that night. Gigs were her life, and sometimes her prison. Some days she would play two or three shows, and some months, forty. Luckily, unlike the marathon Innerchange shows, which went on for upwards of three hours, these shows on the road were trimmed significantly—to under two hours—to preserve Jewel's voice and energy, and get her on the road at a reasonable hour to perform the following night.

"The first night was very hard in each place," said Jenny Price. "There weren't a lot of people, but it was a word-of-mouth thing. She's just so incredibly talented that we knew as soon as she got in front of people, she could win them over."

But, "it didn't happen immediately," said Mike Tallon, owner of the Kendall Cafe in Cambridge, where Jewel did a series of four Sundays in the winter of 1995, shortly before *Pieces of You* was released. "After the first show, I wasn't sure about her," Tallon remembered. "The jury was out." That Sunday, only about thirty-five people turned out to see Jewel, despite a gracious preview in the Boston *Globe*'s weekly calendar section by pop music critic Steve Morse.

The Kendall, with its hundred-person capacity, was typical of the venues Jewel was playing at the time. It had two rooms, with a bar in the front room and a few steps leading to the back room. There, an 8×10 stage was surrounded by walls adorned with posters and signed CDs from the musicians who'd played there, among them Elvis Costello, Pete Droge, and Big Head Todd and the Monsters.

These Sundays at the Kendall were also accompanied by typical New England wintry conditions—blustery and wicked cold. Tallon remembers Jewel took these conditions very seriously, looking like some sort of thrift-store snow bunny desperate to keep warm, bundled to the point of comedy. "She always wore the same reddish coat with white spiky fur around the collar and fur fringes at the bottom." But Tallon admired her tenacity and energy. "She worked her butt off," he said.

Then the word of mouth spread. Fifty people came out from the cold on that second Sunday; seventy-five during week three—mostly college kids, more than half of them women. On the fourth week, 120 people crammed into the club. "The fire marshal would not have approved," Tallon said. The seats were filled, people were standing and sitting on every inch of floor, on tables, on laps. "Eventually we had to stop letting people up the stairs," Talon added.

Sufficiently impressed, Mike Tallon also observed that Jewel's performance was "thoroughly polished. She really connected with the audience. And she played exactly the same way whether the house was small or large."

Jewel developed a great fondness for venues like the Kendall, so much so that when she returned to Boston years later to play the Orpheum, she reminisced about her residency at the Kendall by making up a song—about how bitter cold it was when she'd played there.

The ferocity of Jewel's work ethic at this time created the impression that she was in many places at once. She was laying important groundwork, and she was starting to receive snippets of recognition from the press, even some supporters: Andre Sun, a writer for Toronto's *NOW* magazine, was one of them. Of her performance at Toronto's C'est What Pub in March 1995, he wrote: "She delivers her performance refreshingly free of irony. Catch Jewel at C'est What before she starts appearing on *Spin* magazine covers."

But Sun's optimism was rare in the early days. Mostly, the press ignored or was snide toward Jewel, who wasn't immune to the criticism. She responded in a poem written at an airport cafeteria in June 1995, after reading a bad review:

> *"I think of the scrutiny*
> *and shrink beneath its million eyes*
> *Has she gained weight?*
> *Does blue become her?*
> *Is she losing her light?*
> *Never . . ."*

Often the crowds could be as brutal as the press; sometimes the two would even feed each other. Critics had ridiculed her song "Pieces of You" for being "overly simplistic." Some people at an early Jewel show apparently felt the same way. "I was singing in this coffee shop in Detroit and there were some gay guys over in the corner and they weren't listening to me," Jewel said. "I got to 'faggot,' and they stormed out."

In a way Jewel was lucky that the circumstances of her life had conditioned her not to expect overnight success. By the end of March 1995, without radio or video play, *Pieces of You* was moving only about five hundred copies a week. "Radio stations said my music was unplayable," Jewel said, "and video shows and TV stations said it was unlistenable."

The plan, according to Atlantic's promotion people, was to break Jewel first with high school and college audiences. Jenny Price deliberately kept her away from conventional bookings. She believed that if Jewel was perceived as an adult artist first, younger kids would consider her uncool and would never bother to check her out. From then on, Atlantic reasoned, Jewel would have a hard time escaping the middle of the road.

In addition to a heavy performance schedule, Jewel did promotional interviews, radio and TV appearances, and campus and record store confabs. She would play, sleep a few hours, and drive to the next city. Play and sleep and drive.

As part of the plan to reach kids, Jewel was sometimes booked to play high school assemblies, often early in the morning. This meant pulling apathetic kids out of classes, corralling large groups of boisterous students, and plunking them down in cavernous auditoriums with acoustics reminiscent of airplane hangars. They were difficult crowds at best. However, Jewel's problems were compounded one particular morning by a case of mistaken identity.

No nightmare could have been as vivid as when a crowd of students filed into the Detroit inner-city high school auditorium in high spirits. Jewel peeked through the backstage curtains to find the mostly black student body not only excited, but actually hopped up for her performance. This both confused and elated Jewel. This was a different crowd than she'd ever seen. On the other hand, she was happy the promoter had booked her there. Like any young artist, Jewel hoped to reach every kind of listener.

The thought of winning these kids over, having them accept her with open arms and open minds, sent her reeling with excitement.

The only problem was that this particular crowd thought they were seeing a rap artist named Jewel (pronounced Joo-ELLE). When Jewel walked out, a white girl playing an acoustic guitar, they rebelled, hooting and hollering throughout what would be an abbreviated set. Jewel bravely finished the show, but by the end, most of the kids had walked out.

Jewel's skin was thickening as hostile and indifferent audiences became a common occurrence. If she felt a crowd was being rude, Jewel wasn't afraid to tell them. Her frustration was especially palpable at an Atlantic Records showcase at the 1995 South by Southwest Music Conference in Austin, Texas. Founded in the mideighties and held each March as an independent alternative to New York's New Music Seminar, South by Southwest had become bloated by industry excess. On the verge of its tenth anniversary, it was becoming as overblown as its predecessor. The four-day festival had become an excuse for writers, publicists, A&R people, and label drones to eat too much barbecue, drink too much Shiner Bock, and generally behave badly. Although hundreds of bands played all over town during those four days, the musicians were almost beside the point. South by Southwest was really about getting to the right party, schmoozing in the Four Seasons lobby at three A.M., and ordering chicken-fried steak at Threadgills or ribs at the Iron Works.

When Jewel made her appearance, she faced the most difficult of circumstances. Most of the record labels threw their showcase parties in restaurants like the Green Mesquite, a cozy barbecue joint with an outdoor stage and patio, or in intimate bars like the

Continental Club or Hole in the Wall. But Atlantic somehow chose a ballroom in the Austin Convention Center, where the day's panels and seminars are held. The musicians—who included Melissa Ferrick, Mary Karlzen, and Jill Sobule—all performed alone with acoustic guitars, but had no stage on which to play. Instead, they stood on tables above a room packed with record industry weasels who were more interested in free food. Jewel, playing second, knew what she was up against. The buzzing crowd continued unabated once she started playing. So she stopped. She just stood there, silently. Music had become so beside the point that the crowd only noticed it when it was missing. Eventually people were curious to find out where the silence was coming from. They looked up. And from that tabletop, Jewel scolded the crowd. "They told me you'd be a hard crowd. Now shut up." Guilt, it seems, works with record industry crowds. The buzzing didn't stop completely, but it did quiet to a simmer for the remainder of the twenty-minute set.

Meanwhile, the Atlantic Records promotion machine began rolling. A CD called *Save the Linoleum* was released to radio stations to promote "Who Will Save Your Soul," which was selected as the album's first single. It also featured live and studio outtakes from *Pieces of You*, and included concert favorites like "My Own Private God's Gift to Woman," "I'm Sensitive," "Race Car Driver," and "Flower." Electronic press kits recounting Jewel's movie-of-the-week San Diego Cinderella story were also distributed to the media.

But despite these promotional weapons, Jewel was a tough sell. Atlantic's roster of new artists at the time was woman-heavy. Jewel and her colleagues at the South by Southwest debacle were in some ways competing for attention at the label. Records by Jewel, Jill Sobule, Mary Karlzen, and Melissa Ferrick were all released in early 1995. In many ways they were too similar for differentiation by the public and the media—especially Ferrick,

Karlzen, and Jewel, who each had deep roots in the folk tradition. Many insiders were commenting that when the records came out, it was difficult to tell them apart without lyric sheets. To make matters worse, Atlantic also had Victoria Williams and Juliana Hatfield on its roster, and both had new records out. Much was made of the "Atlantic Women," but it was also easy to get lost in the shuffle. The question was twofold: Which of these women would stand out? Or would none of them?

Victoria Williams had perhaps the most going for her. Though she hadn't sold many records, the press adored her. The Louisiana songwriter with the infectious Southern drawl had been diagnosed with multiple sclerosis three years earlier. Cast in the role of underdog, Williams' *Loose*, released in late 1994, was her first collection of new music since her diagnosis. It was praised highly upon its release. Juliana Hatfield, too, was something of a media darling. Although some thought her star was fading, as a former member of Boston's punk-pop trio the Blake Babies, Hatfield had a large cult following. She had been on the covers of *Sassy* and *Spin*. Claire Danes of the television hit *My So-Called Life* had declared her "my favorite singer." And Hatfield's did-they-or-didn't-they relationship with the Lemonheads' Evan Dando kept her visible on the pop scene.

Jill Sobule's self-titled record was the first of the 1995 Atlantic releases to break out. Her quirky, Cyndi Lauper—esque songwriting sensibility was appealing to listeners, but Sobule also received a lift from the zany, controversial video for her single, "I Kissed a Girl." Featuring he-man Fabio in a cameo role, Sobule got a lot of media attention for the track, as well as steady airplay from MTV. She became a priority for Atlantic.

What about Jewel? Was she a lost cause? Was she just a kid, playing songs that other kids her age weren't into? Jewel's selling point was her back story, that she had lived in a van. Maybe the music could catch up, if she could only hold the public's interest for a little while. Jewel wasn't oblivious to her rank in the label's pecking order. She knew she wasn't snappy or media-friendly or bisexual. She was no darling of the press, like Victoria Williams, nor had she been around long enough to become romantically attached to any rock stars, like Hatfield. In fact, she was considered something of a hot potato internally. After Danny Goldberg left the label at the end of 1994 to become chairman of Mercury Records, Jewel was left without a champion. She wound up being pushed around by members of the Atlantic publicity staff, who complained that she simply wasn't alternative enough.

She eventually fell into the lap of publicist Eileen Thompson, who had held the hand of Paula Abdul during her salad days, as well as guided Wilson Phillips during their hit-making period. She had also handled several corporate accounts while at Rogers & Cowan and later with Atlantic. She knew Jewel would be a tough sell. The young publicist could only make her calls, bite her lip, and hope for the best. During the crucial early stages of the *Pieces of You* campaign, you could count Jewel believers on one hand: Thompson, Jenny Price, and West Coast radio promotion director Kris Metzdorf. Despite the rolled eyes and water cooler jokes, they never stopped believing in the young artist.

Jewel's answer to everything thrown at her during this time was a simple one: Just keep playing. And though she had perceived her grueling coffeeshop tour as a sign that no one had wanted to go on the road with her (Atlantic Records' vice president Ron Shapiro admitted as much), she just kept tuning up, warming up, and playing wherever they sent her. She was tossed before ever more hostile crowds—eventually even as the opening act for cult goth rocker Peter Murphy, formerly of the English band Bauhaus.

For six weeks Jewel walked out alone with an acoustic guitar before an audience that looked like horror movie extras—pasty-looking crowds clad in nothing but black. This was not an audience she could tell to shut up. "I wanted to kill myself after every show," she said. "I'm now sensitive to people who've had their fangs filed." The Peter Murphy experience was just another of many indignities Jewel faced during her first year on the road. At Boston's Beacon Theater, Jewel, awash in hypnotic red lights, began talking about a friend who had died from AIDS. Then, about halfway through her story, some guy in the balcony screamed: "Take it off, Jewel." Unrattled, she smiled, finished her story, and began singing "Pieces of You." This rendition, however, had an extra verse:

> *"Stupid boy*
> *stupid boy*
> *thinks he's smart*
> *he thinks he's cool*
> *in the middle of my show*
> *he shouts, 'take it off, Jewel.' "*

The Boston crowd ate it up; she could do no wrong after that.

Her ability to turn setbacks into gains became a cornerstone of her technique. In Toronto, playing the Opera House, all the lights in the house went out. She still had sound, but the stage was pitch black. Other performers might have panicked or apologized or waited for the situation to remedy itself. Instead, Jewel made the best of it. Here, she thought, was an opportunity to perform without enduring the wolfish gazes of her female fans' boyfriends. She told the crowd, "My face is just a distraction. Let's see how good this sounds in the dark." Her beautiful voice took on an eerie quality, and fans found the experience unforgettable.

Sometimes, though, Jewel's patience wore thin, and she was forced to hold her ground. Playing a summer festival at Robert F. Kennedy Stadium in Washington, D.C., Jewel shared a bill with the Foo Fighters, Gin Blossoms, Everclear, and Afghan

Whigs. She was barely into her second song when a Frisbee hit her in the head. So she stopped playing, looked out at the crowd, offered a terse thank-you, and left the stage. End of show. Through it all, Jewel was a road warrior, never backing down or complaining in the face of difficult circumstances or hard work. Unlike the Grateful Dead, she was not the kind of musician who thrives on a road-goes-on-forever mentality. The infinite self-promotion grew tiresome, constantly having to talk about herself as though she'd never talked the talk before. The endless regurgitation of the same old stories, with no time to herself, wore her thinner and thinner. It tested her faith, but she always reasoned that bad shows and long interviews were better than even one hour of waitressing. Perhaps most important, Jewel believed that her work was of service to others, and that she had a responsibility to go through with it. "I'm learning to like [touring]," she said. "I'm not doing this for fame or money. I'm doing it because it serves my spirit and it reminds people to live their dreams. That's needed in the world now."

During this period of incessant touring, Jewel also found a way to keep growing as an artist, instead of simply becoming more professional. She was always writing new songs and trying them in front of audiences. During her rare downtime she could often be seen scribbling words and phrases on whatever scraps of paper she could get her hands on: matchbook covers, restaurant receipts, book jackets. The stage was her laboratory; the page was her test tube. Playing at San Diego State she sang three new numbers, apparently written only minutes before she took the stage. She plunked the spiral notebook in front of her and referred to it when she couldn't remember the just-composed lyric. Sometimes she would pause to connect the new words to the new melody. And just as they had at the Innerchange, the growing audiences were smitten by the imperfections in Jewel's shows.

"I'm committed to learning in front of the world now, and I'm gonna make mistakes," she said. "I'm gonna do things that aren't brilliant. But I want to make sure I keep growing. I have to take risks to do that, and it's okay if I fall on my face . . . I mean, God, we should be allowed to be human, you know?" Her onstage banter began to evolve as she came to understand the powerful effect humor has on an audience. Her impression of the Cranberries' Dolores O'Riordan was priceless, although Dolores was reportedly unhappy about it. Soon, Jewel's repartee alone became nearly worth the price of admission—a trick she learned from observing the demented storytelling of Steve Poltz back in San Diego. Still, there were issues of balance to be considered, namely that her stage shows misrepresented the work on her album, or vice versa. "A lot of humor comes from the stories I tell and you really can't capture that on an album. I guess you could include banter but it would make for a really long record." But her shows were becoming more and more fun. She would open with something upbeat like "Race Car Driver" before moving, midset, onto more serious material.

Jewel had deliberately kept lighter material like "Race Car Driver" or the yodeling number "Chime Bells" off *Pieces of You* because she knew the power of first impressions and wanted to be taken seriously as a songwriter. "I'm not a very serious person but I'm glad I'm being perceived as more . . . than someone who writes novelty songs," she said.

With the stakes growing higher and venues growing larger, Jewel looked beyond the songs to stage presentation. She experimented with different lighting effects, sometimes opting for a dark, mystical effect on the stage. Often she used pathways of candles which bathed the stage in natural light. Her appearance evolved as well. No longer the homeless teenager in thrift store acquisitions, Jewel looked sharp, dressed in black, and began revealing more of her sexual side through her clothing.

By the spring of 1995, modern rock stations in smaller markets had added "Who Will Save Your Soul" to their playlists. Jewel had taken tiny steps, but they were sufficient to take her to the next level. In May, she opened for Liz Phair at the Wiltern in Los Angeles and the Warfield in San Francisco. These two-thousand-seat theaters were her biggest shows to date. Jewel was particularly nervous about playing with Phair, whom she greatly admired. Phair had opened a lot of eyes with her first record, 1993's *Exile in Guyville,* which was a blunt, song-by-song response to the Rolling Stones' *Exile on Main Street.* 1994's *Whip-Smart* was a solid follow-up.

Jewel was jittery before her first show with Phair. She changed outfits several times, pacing nervously around her dressing room, worried that no one would pay attention to her. Unlike her Peter Murphy shows a few months earlier, Jewel had every reason to believe Liz Phair's audience might respond to her. Along with this expectation came pressure. Jewel said: "I was so scared . . . I thought, how am I going to walk out with an acoustic guitar? I'd been playing small shops and coffeehouses and suddenly I was [about to be] in front of two thousand people. I didn't know if I could pull it off."

Indeed, Jewel was shaky at first, even breaking a pick shortly into the set. Luckily, someone in the audience had an extra, and tossed it up to her. But her forty-minute set picked up steam and ended strongly. The audience reacted enthusiastically enough to call for an encore. And when Jewel she walked back on to the stage, the place was still and quiet. The audience was hers.

By the end of that summer, large stations like WHFS in Washington, D.C., WXRT in Chicago, and WNEW in New York had added "Who Will Save Your Soul" to their playlists. In August alone, twelve thousand copies of *Pieces of You* were purchased. "I got enough of a groundswell to keep playing," Jewel said. "And my label kept me out long enough that people couldn't ignore me anymore. Radio had to start playing the songs." Also, Jewel began to be graced with more compatible touring partners. On the road with Catherine Wheel and Belly, Jewel connected with appropriate audiences, gaining new fans every night. Still, although VH1 had started playing "Who Will Save Your Soul," it was not in regular rotation. Atlantic was getting antsy. They began plans to send Jewel back into the studio in early 1996 and get a record out by the fall. If she was going to make it, they believed, it wasn't going to be with *Pieces of You*.

As part of Jewel's promotional torture, Atlantic tried to squeeze in as many TV appearances for her as possible. In what might have been just another in a series of endless miniperformances, Jewel appeared on *Late Night with Conan O'Brien* in May. At home that night, watching *Conan* on television, was a movie actor by the name of Sean Penn. Immediately, Mr. Penn picked up his phone and tracked Jewel down. He was not only smitten, but clearly impressed. To his friends, Penn began to describe Jewel as "the female Bob Dylan." Suddenly, the Utah-born, Alaska-raised chanteuse wasn't just another musician slogging away on the road. Almost overnight, everyone would know who she was, as the great spotlight in the sky fell upon the young blond girl on the arm of Sean Penn.

CHAPTER SEVEN

Turning a Corner

*You're not learning how to be an artist or a songwriter
anymore, you're learning how to be a smart-minded business
person.*

*T*he Venice Film Festival, perhaps more than any other, is the
stuff of dreams. There are handsome and beautiful movie stars in
Italian tuxedos and ten-thousand-dollar gowns gliding down red
carpets toward thousand-year-old buildings, and behind them the
setting sun shimmers off the Grand Canal. The word *paparazzi*
could have been coined with the media frenzy of this festival in
mind. In Venice, it seems, no one who really wants solitude is
entitled to even a moment of it.

And for a young girl from Alaska, by way of California—who
had been playing her guitar through conditions less thick than
thin, who had seen life from the inside of her own van, from the

postage-stamp stages of the provinces, and only recently from larger halls and better hotels—the paparazzi in Venice must have seemed like some horrible joke, like Cinderella-gone-haywire.

The cameras followed every move made by Jewel and Sean Penn at 1995's Venice Film Festival. Jewel encountered the "Flash! Flash! Smile! Look over here, hon!" every time she stepped from or into a public place, be it a restaurant, cinema, nightclub, or taxi. Worse, though, were the long lenses, which caught her in the private moments when she thought she was alone. The reach of these elaborate cameras made it impossible for Jewel and her new boyfriend, movie-star Sean, to lose themselves in the culture and exoticism of a foreign land. To be alone the couple stayed in their room, and that caused a great deal of talk. Everywhere they went, people stared and pointed.

So this was fame. The experience gave her pause, and she had second thoughts about the trajectory of her career after brushing all too close against the dark, sordid side of the unrelenting press. But by now, it was already too late.

Jewel was involved only briefly with Sean Penn. After a short separation he resumed his involvement with actress Robin Wright, and married her.

Although their tryst was short and sweet ("It was what it was, but compared to the duration of other relationships I've had, it's not a big deal"), Jewel's tenure with Penn put an end to her relationship with Steve Poltz, her mentor. It was also a shot in the arm for her career. When the affair became public, in late summer 1995, Jewel was a young musician trying to make a name for herself. Months of touring couldn't possibly have had the impact of appearing on the arm of a movie star at a film festival like Venice; Jewel would never be confused with Melissa Ferrick again. If Sean Penn declared her "the new Dylan," why, she must be an artist worth checking out. Suddenly, cultural tastemakers like *Rolling Stone* magazine were putting Jewel in their Random Notes section.

Penn also proved a wise teacher, explaining to Jewel the ropes of media management. After doing probation for attacking a photographer in his younger days, the actor had since mellowed, and had acquired a unique perception of fame and the media. Penn told her just how much of herself she needed to reveal to the press, and he explained that it's perfectly fine to offer tiny pieces rather than large, soul-baring chunks. The Penn connection paid other dividends, as well. He commissioned her to contribute a song to *The Crossing Guard,* a film starring Jack Nicholson that Penn directed. The film was released during 1995's holiday season, and included Jewel's song "Emily" in its soundtrack. The song was a melancholy one, about losing faith in life. "Where does love go / if it can't find a home / one moment here then gone," Jewel sings with poignancy.

Of course, Jewel's dalliance with Penn had a down side: namely, Jewel found herself barraged with questions about herself and the actor long after the relationship ended. And she was visibly uncomfortable having to answer them. "People like to speculate," she said of the public's tendency to inhale headlines from the tabloid press. "It feels like they're talking about someone else. It doesn't even feel real to me." But around this time, Jewel also began to experience the phenomenon of suddenly knowing many fewer people than those who claim to know her: "When people hear intimate things in my music, they think it makes us best friends somehow. In a way that's true, but in a way it's not true at all . . . I don't consider myself a particularly private person, [but] we all have things that are meant for our family and friends. They have pieces of you that you don't give to other people."

By the fall of 1995, Atlantic sensed that "Who Will Save Your Soul" was tapped out as a single. They quickly released "You Were

Meant for Me," which Jewel co-wrote with Steve Poltz, as the second radio track from *Pieces of You*. And since Penn was eager to work with Jewel, he proposed that he direct the video. Atlantic agreed, only after making the actor/director jump through a few hoops—he was asked to submit a reel of his work (by this time, Penn had already directed the motion picture *The Indian Runner*). Shortly thereafter, Penn prepared a budget of $80,000 for the "You Were Meant for Me" video—an inconsequential sum for an artist like, say, Michael Jackson, but for Jewel it was something of an extravagance. Ultimately, the single was a failure, and no one was eager to play the video.

At this point, Atlantic executives began grumbling. They once again threatened to throw in the towel on *Pieces of You* and send Jewel into the studio for a follow-up album for early 1996. But, once again, an angel was standing by Jewel. She caught another break with a flurry of high-profile television appearances late in the year. VH1, an early supporter, offered Jewel a slot with Melissa Etheridge on its prestigious *Duets* program. Jewel performed "Foolish Games" and the unreleased "Sleep While I Drive."

Broadcast on TNT the very same night as *Duets* came Jewel's performance as Dorothy in a benefit production of *The Wizard of Oz* for the Children's Defense Fund at New York's Lincoln Center. Jewel was in good company that night, as the cast of actors and musicians included Roger Daltrey as the Tin Man, Jackson Browne as the Scarecrow, Debra Winger as the Wicked Witch, Nathan Lane as the Cowardly Lion, Natalie Cole as Glinda the Good Witch, Joel Grey as the Wizard, and Lucie Arnaz as Auntie Em, and all were backed up by the Boys Choir of Harlem. Scenes from the film were performed, along with its entire score—including songs deleted from the 1939 movie.

"She had a certain innocence," said *Oz* executive producer Jonathan Brauer. It had been Jewel's first acting gig since her days at Interlochen, but, as always, she approached the role with fearlessness. "The part was given to me off an interview I did on [National Public Radio's] *All Things Considered,*" Jewel said. "[Executive producer Brauer] had never heard me sing and he'd never seen me act. He just liked my ideas, and I thought, 'what an opportunity.'

"I showed up for rehearsals five days before the show and it was all very thrown together," she added. "It was a big mouthful to have that big of a script and to have two dance routines, but if water seeks its own level, I couldn't go wrong because all you can do is rise to the occasion." Jewel said the highlight of the show for her was doing a guitar duet with legendary ax man Ry Cooder on "Over the Rainbow."

Less than a week after *Wizard* aired, Jewel was again on the couch next to Conan O'Brien on late night. Soon, scores of magazines were writing small articles about the singer. Atlantic had momentum, and a new sales goal: 200,000. The label decided that the youth market had been sewn up and it was now time to focus on adults. To that end, she was booked on virtually every national television talk show currently running. She appeared on *Entertainment Tonight* in December and *The Tonight Show with Jay Leno* the day after Christmas. And, reinforcing their revitalized commitment, Atlantic rereleased "Who Will Save Your Soul" as a single—this time a rerecorded version with a fuller, radio-friendly sound.

This would prove just the ticket to get Jewel on the radio, as the song became a top ten hit, peaking at number two on VH1. When it was added in early 1996 to Los Angeles' KROQ—the most influential modern rock station in the country—the rest of the nation followed suit. By the spring, she was finally embraced by MTV, where she hosted *Alternative Nation* and appeared as a guest on *120 Minutes*. Around this time, Jewel kicked off her first headlining tour (dubbed the Tiny Lights Tour), playing clubs with a three-piece band. It was an intense, heady time.

By the time *Pieces of You went* gold in mid-1996, Jewel figured she'd spent no more than two weeks at her new San Diego apartment. "I've toured my butt off for a year and a half and my fans have been so loyal that MTV can't ignore it anymore," she said. And even when she saw the chance for daylight, she couldn't be bothered to slow down her ferocious pace. One morning she taped a segment for MTV in Colorado, got on an airplane, and performed that night before a crowd of five thousand in Durham, North Carolina—prompting a local radio disc jockey to call her "the hardest working woman in pop." In response, Jewel was heard saying: "I was made for what I do. Some horses are workhorses and some are race horses. I'm a show horse." Jewel's love of performance, brought about by her ability to forge a close connection with an audience, cannot be overestimated. Never shy about revealing her emotions on stage and never forgetting where she was and how she got there, at a May 1996 show at New York's Irving Plaza, she blurted out, "I love my life." And, by that point, what was not to love?

She was always trying to get better—write better songs, play better guitar, be better on stage. At the same time, her growing fame had not changed her tendency to take risks. "I want to change and grow," she said. "I'm not perfect and I'm not going to portray myself in some polished slick image . . . We're human, we do the best we can." She also admits, "I make plenty of mistakes and get criticized for being young and naive—it's okay, I am . . . as long as you have the spark of emotion and speak from your own heart, you move the hearts of other people—that's a very noble gift."

It should be mentioned that Jewel's "noble gift" had not gone unnoticed by Atlantic executives like Ron Shapiro. "The record industry was in the toilet when Jewel came around," says *USA Today* writer Bruce Haring, whose book, *Off the Charts,* offers a not-so-rosy look at the machinations of the record industry. "Around that time, Atlantic executives decided to focus on a handful of acts, like Jewel and Hootie and the Blowfish, rather than continuing to spread their money around." Haring contends that Atlantic has spent so much money in promotional support of Jewel that even after selling eight million copies of *Pieces of You* they haven't recouped their investment. "Give her champions credit," says Haring, "Jenny [Price], Danny [Goldberg], and Ron Shapiro, for sticking with Jewel's course."

Notwithstanding Jewel the performer, Jewel the businesswoman couldn't help but be cynical about being played by radio stations who wouldn't have given her the time of day six months earlier. "Every aspect of the business that I've seen is 'Follow the Leader,'" she said. "Nobody has courage . . . [except] the people who believed in me at Atlantic."

Another believer was Jewel's mother, Nedra, who savvily kept Jewel on track. Although new to this world, Nedra was a quick study. "The whole artist development thing, how a young artist develops in particular, is something I pay a lot of attention to. The industry doesn't always," Nedra has said. "I think it's very difficult to grow in a way that's satisfying unless you have the right support system. It doesn't have to be a parent, but you need a team—legal, management, record company—to support you. Self-confidence and moxie help, too."

But all that means nothing unless an artist connects with her audience and has a base of fans. Jewel's fans, going back to her Innerchange days, supported her unconditionally, with a devotional fervor. She explains her ability to tour incessantly by the continued intensity of her fans. "They've really kept my spirits up. They bootleg my stuff. Their goal is to get all my material," Jewel said. "It's good because I write a lot of new stuff and I forget 'em. If it wasn't for my fans sending me back the bootlegs, the stuff would be gone forever."

Jewel often likes to keep her listeners on their toes. "I think you have to layer your work, put in stuff for people to find down the line," Jewel has said. "If you don't, well, that shoots longevity in the foot." Case in point: When Jewel went back on the road in early 1996, she found herself opening for fellow Atlantic recording artist Edwin McCain. By this time, Jewel had total control of her audience. Her once long-winded stories had become to-the-point, funny, and captivating; she took the time to explain the origins of songs like "Daddy" and "Painters." She took requests, broke a pick (which was becoming a ritual), and got a new one from the audience. The tide was definitely turning; a Seattle newspaper reporter questioned why the bill wasn't the other way around. The critic marveled at Jewel's ability to change her voice from that of an innocent child to that of a somber woman. When Jewel left the stage, half the crowd left as well.

Put very simply, Jewel's fans love her. And thanks to the international reach of the Internet, she has an on-line fan club mobilized under the moniker Everyday Angels (jewel@smoe.org maillist). The club appropriated its name from Jewel's I-can-do-anything anthem "I'm Sensitive":

> "Anyone can start a conflict
> It's harder yet to disregard
> I'd rather see the world from another angle
> We are everyday angels
> Be careful with me 'cause I'd like to stay that way."

Via E-mail, Jewel fans, who have nicknames like "The Little Angel," "The Distant Angel," "The Angel Who Thinks Too Much," "The Angel Formerly Known As . . . ," discuss melodies, lyrics, TV appearances, concerts, Jewel's hair color, costume choices, and career decisions. They trade tapes (Jewel's live recordings are called "Angelfood" by fans), memorabilia, and anything else Jewel-related. The Jewel fan phenomenon is like nothing else in popular music, except, perhaps for the Grateful Dead and its Deadheads. These fans come in all ages, colors, and nationalities, with very little in common other than a sincere admiration for Jewel and her music. And these fans pour their hearts out.

One fan, an aspiring young poet, posted on E-mail that she had just been selected for publication in a journal called *Rhymes and Greatness*. "Jewel has been the biggest inspiration in my life," the poet claims. Another fan remembers going with a friend to see Juliana Hatfield at a Toronto radio station in March of 1995. Ironically, it was Jewel, singing in the studio, who they remember seeing. "I was in awe. This beautiful girl could sing!" the fan remembers. Afterward, she and her friend waited to get Jewel's autograph, expecting the singer to scribble her name and move swiftly along. Instead, Jewel took the time to meet them, learn their names, and invite them to her show that evening at the C'est What Pub.

The same fan ran into Jewel at C'est What before the show—in the bathroom of all places. Nervous about disturbing the singer before she performed, she was also concerned that Jewel, who had been so personable earlier in the day, wouldn't remember having met her. Not only did Jewel remember her, Jewel seemed really excited to see her and thanked her sincerely for coming. Since then, she reports, at every Jewel show she attends, the singer always takes the time to chat warmly with fans before and after shows.

Jewel's biggest fans embrace her as much for the inspiration she provides as the music she creates. A college freshman in the midwest, who felt that his own life plans did not correspond to those that his parents had mapped out for him, said on the Everyday Angels list that learning about Jewel's decision to follow her dreams gave him hope: "She makes me believe that maybe I could be strong enough to do that too. . . ." These stories all have a common refrain: Jewel, more than most performers, and certainly more than most famous ones, remembers where she came from and how she traveled.

Jewel regards her fans so highly that sometimes their wish is her command—as was the case when the Everyday Angels were special guests at a private performance, by their favorite artist. It began as a "wish upon a star" from E-mail list member Anita Martin, who mused, "Wouldn't it be cool if Jewel did a show just for us?" The wish, and ensuing performance, took place while Jewel was riding high on the rerelease of "Who Will Save Your Soul." She was spending some time recording during the summer of 1996, cutting tracks at Woodstock's legendary Bearsville Studios. Produced by Peter Collins, best known for his work with Genesis, this material would ostensibly appear on her second album. She was holed up cutting, among others, "Satellite," with her pal Flea, the bassist from the Red Hot Chili Peppers, when Jewel agreed to do a free show for her Internet fans, provided they could make it up to Woodstock.

Mike Connell and Richard Chang, fans from the Woodstock area, were the point people, relaying information to Everyday Angels throughout the country. Fans established Web sites and initiated a travel system ("Angel Needs a Ride," naturally) to get people up to Woodstock. T-shirts were designed, plans wer~ swiftly made, and the event eventually took on a life of its own. Originally planned as a single, private performance, an additional show was added, with the second to benefit the theater where it was held.

Dubbed Jewelstock, the shows were held July 18 and 19, 1996, at the intimate Bearsville Theatre. Patty Griffin opened the show. And Jewel, committed to giving her special fans—the hardest of the hardcore—what they wanted, played the least common material. Many of the songs did not appear on *Pieces of You,* but were only familiar to those who listened to Angelfood tapes. Needless to say, "Who Will Save Your Soul" was not performed. It was a loose, playful event where Jewel read her poems and gave herself over to the audience's requests. After the show she hung out with the several hundred fans in attendance, some of whom had come from as far away as California, to chat, sign autographs, and pose for pictures.

While always appreciative of her fans, she's careful to take their attentions in stride. "To have people idolize you is strange because it half-flatters you. You want to pretend that it says something about you," she said. "But if you believe [the flattery], you become relative to it. Then you're only as good as your last compliment or critique." Despite a schedule that would overwhelm even the heartiest of souls, Jewel continues to write a new song every week. She also never neglects to find ten minutes a day to sit alone with her guitar.

The material Jewel recorded at Bearsville was initially scheduled to come out as a second album in April 1997. Like the Stray Gators on the *Pieces of You* studio sessions, the new record included a stellar lineup of musicians: bassist T-Bone Wolk from the *Saturday Night Live* house band, who has worked with Hall and Oates and Elvis Costello; percussionist Michael Blair, who worked with Lou Reed; drummer Jerry Marotta; and guitarist Marc Schulman. There was no problem finding enough material to fill another record, either: Jewel had scores of songs, along with a stack of books of scribbled poetry that could be converted into songs.

But no second record would come so soon—thanks to the fact that *Pieces of You* had taken off and wouldn't die. The music business is like any other: If it ain't broke, don't fix it. Sales of *Pieces of You* continued to outpace all expectations, thanks largely to Jewel's tireless touring, which by summer '96 included the modern rock festival circuit. With much larger crowds, headlining shows, and with considerable press attention, it was a far cry from the modesty and cramped confines of eighteen months earlier. "I'm looking back on some of the gigs I've done, going, 'How did I do it?' " Jewel recalled in 1996. "In Philadelphia . . . I [played] in a coffee shop that had a stage . . . like a little postage stamp . . . everybody talked and you couldn't make people listen by screaming." Things were very different at the Y100 Shindig in Philadelphia. Jewel was more comfortable for one thing, and her considerably larger audience watched, rapt, as Jewel started her forty-minute set with "Pieces of You." Then, during the "faggot" verse, she poked fun at the Cranberries' Dolores O'Riordon and Keanu Reeves, telling the audience that her fantasy was to have Dolores come onstage, wearing a wedding dress which exposed her belly button. Keanu would be behind her, carrying her train to prove he wasn't gay. Delores would then sing "faggot, faggot" to the tune of "Zombie."

She also likes to go with the flow. One of the highlights of that summer was a gig at the Tibetan Freedom Festival in the San Francisco Bay area, organized by the Beastie Boys' Mike D. As has been the case many times with Jewel, she was forced to find the silver lining after discovering she'd been offered a cloud. Resplendent on the main stage in a gold miniskirt, Jewel was doing battle with the band currently playing on the second stage. Rather than get upset, however, her response was to ask the people situated on the lawn of Mountain View's Shoreline Amphitheater to come down and get closer. When they did, she told them: "I can't believe I'm in front of all you people . . . it's because you guys buy my album that I get to eat." By this time, of course, she could do more than merely eat—she was now a platinum-selling recording artist.

Still, for those who think she's rolling in dough, Jewel has a quick response. "People think you have money," Jewel said. "And it's frustrating because you're still starving . . . but [the record company advance] is a loan. You owe it back to them, with interest." It's undeniable, of course, that Jewel is a hot commodity, and it's impossible for her to please everyone. It broke Jewel's heart to break a commitment to appear at the Alaska State Fair in July '96. Touring prevented her from making good on her earlier promise to appear, and her nonperformance was something of a cause célèbre, angering the fair's organizers, upset that they had spent $10,000 on publicity to promote the homecoming of Alaska's favorite daughter. "If you can't trust someone from Homer, who can you trust?" said marketing director Dean Phipps.

At least Jewel stayed busy serving her country, or at least covering one of her country's biggest events—the Democratic National Convention—for MTV. While her performance as a correspondent will probably not make Diane Sawyer quake in her boots, Jewel's finger was squarely on the pulse of young America. And, unlike the ABC correspondent, Jewel found it hard to show journalistic detachment while reporting on Aretha Franklin's singing of the national anthem. "Oh, my god. Aretha Franklin. I'm such a fan. The queen. One day, when I grow up, maybe I'll be half as good as Aretha."

In light of Jewel's success, her modesty is even more impressive. The girl who once described herself as "a big dork of rock and roll," still keeps her head squarely on her shoulders: "I'm not hip and I'm not a coolster. I'm just a kid with an acoustic guitar who keeps slinging it out." Well, maybe she's just a kid, but she's slinging it out next to some serious heavyweights. After recording at Bearsville, Jewel was back on the road with a full band, this time with Neil Young and Crazy Horse. Only months earlier she had opened for Bob Dylan on his "never-ending" tour. "Neil is incredible," Jewel said. "And touring with Bob Dylan was a huge dream." She also shared a stage with him, trading vocals on "I Shall Be Released." Backstage, Dylan asked her to recite some of the lyrics to her songs, but Jewel was too embarrassed. She wasn't, however, too embarrassed to tweak Dylan's nose onstage during one of their performances together. It would become yet another chapter in the growing Jewel legend.

By the end of the year, Jewel could look back at 1996 as the twelve months when all her dreams came true. *Pieces of You* had sold more than two million copies, and the accolades were rolling in. Though the runaway success of her debut put the release of her second album on hold, her fans could still find pieces of Jewel all over the place: She covered Donovan's "Sunshine Superman" on the *I Shot Andy Warhol* soundtrack and John Hiatt's "Have a Little Faith in Me" on the *Phenomenon* soundtrack; "Under the Water" appears on the *Craft* soundtrack. She also recorded with Steve Poltz's Rugburns, singing backup on "My Old Lover's House" on their album *Taking the World by Donkey.*

Jewel won an MTV video award for the post–Sean Penn version of "You Were Meant for Me," which featured Steve Poltz in a prominent role. Then she was nominated for two Grammy Awards, for Best New Artist and Best Female Pop Vocal Performance on "Who Will Save Your Soul." Jewel summed it up very simply: "It's amazing what happens when you focus your brain on something."

The Grammys would be held in early 1997, and though she wouldn't win one, by all rights that night should have been Jewel's crowning moment, her coming-out party for the world. Instead, she would once again feel the stabbing of the sharp pens and tongues of the press. All over a silly dress.

CHAPTER EIGHT

Crown Jewel

I think cream rises to the top. You do it because you love it, not for fame.

The 1997 Grammy Awards seemed like an appropriate occasion for Jewel to let her hair down. After all, she was there to celebrate two nominations: Best New Artist, and Best Female Pop Vocal Performance for "Who Will Save Your Soul."

It was Jewel's moment. And though she lost in both categories, she managed to shine beyond her wildest expectations. Perhaps no double loser in Grammy history has come away with such a flourish.

That night, Jewel wore a sheer, sexy white gown—one that revealed more than a few pieces of the artist. In fact, under the bright television lights you could pretty much see all of the amply endowed Alaskan. The next day, Jewel and her dress were prominent in post-Grammy coverage. The dress could be found in magazine and newspaper photographs and on television videotape. It would be mentioned around watercoolers in offices around the nation. It became the source of catty commentary. And though Jewel's increased penchant for glamour had been ignored by the press and public, her manager, Inga Vainshtein, had been agressively cultivating this awareness in the young artist since the Innerchange days.

Jewel was smart enough to understand her popularity was due largely to the sincerity of her music, coupled with the imperfections of her appearance—the crooked teeth and nose—and the storybook qualities of her life. People could relate to this image of Jewel. Through that image she touched millions of lives. Jewel had been painted in the media as a righteous young earthchick, but she was no longer just a teenager in a van. She was twenty-two, a multiplatinum artist. When she went out for the evening, she liked to dress up.

She was not amused by all the attention, and in a moment of frustration she remarked, "How could I have known the dress was see-through? My hotel room wasn't backlit!" She was disappointed at the uproar over her sexuality, that the public couldn't simply accept her desire to play music from her heart. Overnight, Jewel had become a sex symbol. Ironically she had achieved this by riding the crest of the wave of her own sincerity.

Jewel countered this by continuing to be sincere: "If people are trying to be sexy in an insincere way, you can tell," she said. "Women are beautiful and sensual—we are. People, especially Americans, can be very uptight about that. Which is their trip, not mine."

Ah, fame. Jewel's dream came true in 1997, but at a high price. She was learning quickly that where the media is concerned, every aspect of the life of a public figure is fair game. Whenever it all seemed overwhelming, she remembered what Sean Penn once told her: "Fame is an adjustment worth making."

"Fame . . . is something you experience through other people's perceptions of you . . . [W]hen I was living in my car, people didn't believe in me. Now that I'm famous, people do. But . . . I've always been me." Fame has brought Jewel a lack of privacy. Everyone would like a piece of her now—and though she handles these pressures with as much poise as could reasonably be expected— sometimes all she wants is a little solitude. "As a girl I used to go out in the meadows and pray," she said. "Now, because my days are so full with people and meetings, I go into the bathroom to be alone. It's the last sacred place." And if she can't find a bathroom, she pulls out a small Tupperware container filled with soil from her home in Alaska. "When it starts getting too thick I just open it and smell the earth," she said.

Jewel was barely out of her teens when *Pieces of You* was released in 1995. In her twenties now, she's evolving and growing as a person and as an artist. But, of course, her growth is being scrutinized and dissected by a world of fans and critics. Jewel remains, as usual, undaunted, even defiant, about this kind of pressure. "Poetry is the snakeskin of the soul. You're going to watch my evolution," she said. "I know what I can do in my head, and I've always been able to rise to challenges."

The challenge for Jewel in 1997 was to maintain her grace under the spotlight, even as she was anointed the It Girl of pop music. Maybe she even expected that the year would be some kind of a magic carpet ride after she was invited to perform at one of President Clinton's inaugural balls. Of course, it didn't hurt that first daughter Chelsea had specifically requested Jewel's presence. And although Jewel was active in the Rock the Vote campaign, she is admittedly far from a policy wonk. "I never considered myself to be particularly politically oriented," she said. But she continued: "However, we are all humans. We all live here."

Her star power is such that by the time she appeared on the

debut segment of VH1's *Hard Rock Live*, the entire episode was devoted to her performance, even though she was scheduled to share the show with Rusted Root. That night's show was especially memorable as she yodeled with Atz and sang a tender rendition of "Rudolph the Red-Nosed Reindeer" with Nedra. Jewel was transported to dinner table singalongs and Alaskan hotel lounges. It was like old times.

But every time she returned to the road, she'd see how much had changed, even in two short years. In March 1997, she sold out the Berkeley Community Theater, two years after playing before crowds that numbered fewer than twenty. At this particular show a fan shouted: "I love you, Jewel." She became flustered, blew a chord, stopped, and smiled an exasperated smile. "I know, but I hate it when you do that."

She also headlined the Wiltern Theater in Los Angeles where, in 1995, she had nervously opened for Liz Phair. This time she played for ninety minutes and the critics raved about the confidence she'd gained; all the girlish giddiness that characterized earlier performances, they reported, were cast aside. And the crowd was ever more smitten. Mostly young and female, they clung to every lyric, as their heroine performed vocal gymnastics that rivaled divas like Whitney Houston and Mariah Carey.

After two years of crisscrossing the world, Jewel still found a sense of peace on the stage singing her songs. "[Performing] feeds me . . . allows me to be sincere in an arena that isn't particularly sincere," she said. "I think cream rises to the top . . . [you] do it because you love it, not for fame."

But still, occasional downs tempered the ups. The winter of 1997 brought Jewel to Europe. On one hand, she was chosen to perform at the Nobel Prize ceremony in Sweden; on the other hand, while in Germany, touring with Willie "Cadillac Walk" DeVille, Jewel had a Peter Murphy flashback. To DeVille's fans, eight million records didn't mean diddly. Jewel proved she could take the punch. "His crowds are so mean to me," she said. "I've never played such tough crowds. It's a humbling business. It feels good because fame is only in other people's minds. It's not a reality."

Jewel's breakthrough into the stratosphere was marked by a cover profile in *Rolling Stone* in May, following an *MTV Unplugged* special and an appearance on *Saturday Night Live*. Then, just when she thought she couldn't get higher, Sarah McLachlan organized the Lilith Fair. It was the perfect exclamation point to the success women were having on the pop charts: Meredith Brooks' "Bitch," Paula Cole's "Where Have All the Cowboys Gone," and Sheryl Crow's "If it Makes You Happy" among them. McLachlan headlined the tour, of course, but Jewel was the show's hottest commodity, now with a third single, "Foolish Games," in the upper reaches of the charts. The song followed the pattern of her previous hits: it was rerecorded and beefed up for radio. "Foolish Games" also enjoyed the added exposure of having been featured on the *Batman and Robin* soundtrack.

In the Year of the Woman, Jewel was the Woman of the Year. The Lilith Fair must have come as a relief—the chance to hang back and groove on the other performers. There was no need to carry the event on her back, and it was fun to share the road with fellow travelers after the long and lonely tours of the past twenty-eight months. The Lilith Fair shows were a celebration: At the end of each show, all the evening's performers converged onstage to pay homage to Joni Mitchell—by singing her exuberant ode to the evils of progress, "Big Yellow Taxi."

"I'm happy right now. I feel it's a good time to be a singer/

songwriter," Jewel said while on the tour. "I think women have the innate ability to emote . . . [and the fans] seem to be responding to honesty." Love had replaced the snarl of cynicism. Scores of so-called experts told McLachlan that her tour would never fly, that a bill with only women wouldn't sell tickets. It was derided as the "breast fest" and "lesbo-palooza," yet when the summer concert season ended, Lilith was its most successful tour. Still, Jewel did take exception to *Time* magazine's headline in August, when she appeared on the cover: "Jewel and the Gang." "I'm glad that the tour's gotten noticed," Jewel said. "At the same time, I just think it's silly to call us a gang . . . [were] Nirvana and Pearl Jam and Soundgarden [when they played Lollapalooza] ever called a gang?"

Though the press eventually sharpened their pens on the tour, pointing out its lack of musical diversity and dearth of men (of all things!), the fans certainly came away satisfied. One twelve-year-old shared her Lilith Fair experience on the Internet, writing that she met Jewel in August. It was the fourth time she had seen Jewel, but it was special because she also brought her best friend and her six-year-old sister. It was her sister's first-ever rock show; she had been "asking for weeks if we could meet Jewel after the concert." After the show ended, the girls stopped at the backstage area and identified themselves as members of the Everyday Angels fan club. They asked if they could say hello to Jewel.

"Finally, we decided to pray to our angels in hopes that maybe Jewel would get the message," the fan wrote. "[My friend] promised to never smoke a single cigarette if she got to meet Jewel." The heavens opened: A security guard led them backstage, down a corridor, right to their hero. Jewel smiled as the girls gave her hugs and kisses. "It was like Jewel totally surrounded us in love," she wrote. Jewel signed their T-shirts, drawing angels, and writing, "You are loved, Jewel."

But for Jewel, expressing kindness to fans is the least she can do. Even though she's one of the biggest pop stars in America, she still sees herself as a struggling waitress eating off people's plates. Jewel never forgets the hard times, but proposes: "Optimism is a choice . . . Innocence isn't ever really lost; we just need to maintain it . . . I know the fame might come and go, the money can come and go. But I'm really interested . . . in keeping it aligned to a certain kind of integrity with which I can face each day."

1998 promised to be another magical year for Jewel, as the world finally looked forward to hearing a brand-new full-length studio recording. To be sure, Jewel was more comfortable in the studio now, a far cry from the girl who once compared singing in the studio to faking an orgasm. But most of the tracks she laid down in 1996 at Bearsville Studios did not even make the cut. Since then, she'd written a slew of new songs, and her studio skills improved every day.

In 1996, Jewel wondered if she'd get to record another record. By late 1997 she was talking about the long haul and maintaining her creative edge for life, hoping to have the kind of career that marked some of rock's most important figures. "There are certain people who have never lost the creative integrity of what they're doing. Neil Young, Bob Dylan, Paul Simon. I find people like that very inspiring."

And perhaps as a test of her creative integrity, Jewel chose the least likely of venues to ring in 1998: Las Vegas, a town full of sin. After all, what's a young proponent of inspiration doing in Vegas, that desert mirage created by mobsters fifty years ago? It's a place where they take your money, shatter your dreams, and break your spirit. It's nothing if not a Technicolor metaphor for America's rambling, gambling past; a mythical Wild West where anything goes. The possibilities—if you manage to win—are limitless. But if you're looking for a soul, forget about it—it won't be found in Vegas. It seems the last place in the world you'd find Jewel Kilcher, self-declared antithesis of glitter gulch. Yet here she was, sending off 1997 with a performance at the Hard Rock Casino.

Look a little deeper, however, and you'll find that Jewel actually has much in common with Las Vegas. Certainly, she took a gamble with her life, risking everything to become a working singer/songwriter. And, though it took a while, she came up with sevens. With dogged persistence and years of touring, of dropping quarter after quarter, she became a pop queen.

If you think about it, there's nothing Vegas likes more than a winner, and Jewel was among the biggest ones of 1997. Her New Year's Eve engagement was the culmination of a remarkable three-year run, the last phase of the world's extended introduction to an artist who, not too many moons ago, was just another homeless troubadour singing for her supper. Besides, Jewel isn't known to back down from a challenge. If anyone could tame a roomful of drunken revelers, it was this girl who had melted the hearts of a nation with her hopeful, poetic tunes, and who almost single-handedly snapped pop music out of its cynical malaise.

Las Vegas needed snapping out of its malaise, as well. The town had come a long way from $3.99 prime rib and five-cent slot machines. This wasn't your grandmother's Las Vegas. This was Luxor and New York, not the tired Sands—the perennial favorite of Sinatra's Rat Pack—which had been demolished a year earlier. Cheap buffets and geriatric comics like Buddy Hackett and Don Rickles weren't going to pack the punch needed to lure the Generation Xers, or even the Baby Boomers. In short, Vegas was staring at a midlife crisis. The answer: a little nineties razzmatazz and a lot of cosmetic surgery. The marketing geniuses came up with the ultimate contradiction: turn the town into a family destination. Never mind that gambling is illegal to those under eighteen, and that there's little else to do but gamble in Vegas. The city added a few roller coasters and built like crazy.

As the complexion of the strip and the rehabilitation of downtown Vegas transformed the town, the stigma of playing Vegas also changed. Long considered a graveyard for rock 'n' roll performers, suddenly Vegas was a regular stop on every band's touring itinerary. Playing Vegas was now most cool in a postmodern sort of way.

Thus there wasn't much eyebrow-raising (except from her Internet fans, the Everyday Angels) when Jewel was booked to headline the Hard Rock on December 31, 1997. And she wasn't alone: She was merely one of several rock-based performers at the Hard Rock that night, including teenage blues hotshot Johnny Lang and Orange County metalheads Sugar Ray. Judging by the bulging casinoful of slick-haired hipsters and slinkily attired babes making their way from table to table, it was the It Place to see the It Girl on the It Night.

She had a premonition that this would not be the easiest of shows. That afternoon, while doing leg lifts in the Hard Rock's fitness room, a fan struck up a conversation with her about the night's show. "Tell everyone to shut up for me," Jewel told the fan. She waved good-bye, put on a pair of purple velvet sweatpants, and with bodyguard in tow, made her way to the elevator, back to her room. And shortly before showtime, Jewel told Steve Poltz, whose Rugburns were opening, not to play a rowdy show. The idea was to keep the hoi polloi at bay.

By 9:30 on New Year's Eve, the casino was all ching-ching-ching, abuzz with gamblers and partiers—only a fraction lucky enough to snag tickets to Jewel's ten o'clock show at the Joint, a 1,500-seat club at the far end of the hotel's lobby. To be sure, it wasn't a casinoful of Everyday Angels, but it certainly felt different from most casinos in Las Vegas. Unlike the Mirage or

Bally's, the Hard Rock was teeming with youth, drawn to the giant glowing guitar in the parking lot; drawn to the promise of rock 'n' roll; to the vintage Jimi Hendrix guitar in the lobby, or the costumes Madonna wøre on her Blond Ambition tour. This was the new Vegas, and these people were here to have a good time.

Too good, in some cases. More than two hours before midnight, the casualties were stumbling or being carried out the door. These lightweights and brave souls got too early a start. The casino began to feel like a boat on a stormy sea, and the show hadn't even begun. When the Rugburns—Steve Poltz, bassist John Castro, and drummer Jim Castro—hit the stage shortly after ten, they were met with indifference, even after opening with the humorous and delightful "Chair Song." Lost on many of these fans was the significance of the Poltz-Jewel pairing. Despite their ups and downs, Poltz remained Jewel's biggest supporter and mentor. Jewel tried to return the favor whenever possible, frequently hiring the Rugburns as her opening act. Only a few weeks before, at the Belly Up in San Diego, it seemed like a carnival when Jewel had hopped onstage with the band, joining in on a few tunes.

Tonight was no carnival, however. Sensing the incessant buzz in the audience, Poltz directed the band to plow through their set at warp speed. Several songs passed before Poltz attempted to charm the crowd with the banter that had helped make him a fixture in San Diego for more than a decade.

Jewel made her way to the stage during the Rugburns' finale, the cutesy doo-wop number "Impala." She sidled up to the microphone and traded lovey-dovey verses with Poltz—hardly a dramatic entrance, she just sorta showed up. The startled crowd rubbed their collective eyes, and then it hit them . . . there . . . she . . . is.

She was resplendent as the Woman in Black—snug satin

trousers and a cleavage-revealing spaghetti-strap top. No buildup, no star trip. The biggest pop star in America just quietly appeared. It was all very casual. Especially in Vegas. Just as Jewel wanted it. The Rugburns, sans Poltz, stayed on stage for the opening number, a solid rendition of her signature hit, "Who Will Save Your Soul." They left the stage and, alone, Jewel sang the title track from *Pieces of You*.

Jewel spun a typically witty yarn—this one about doing a show at a modeling convention, surrounded by bulimic supermodels, afraid to touch their food. "Jean-Luc Picard was there up front," Jewel explained from the stage. "And when I got to the 'faggot' part of *Pieces of You*, he just about dropped his fork." It was vintage Jewel, and many laughed.

Some were oblivious, however, and Jewel took to scolding the audience: "I don't mind having you thrown out and refunding your money," she told the ever-milling crowd. They quieted down and she proceeded to play her heart out, without wasted gestures or banter. Flea came onstage and accompanied Jewel on "Satellite." At virtually any other show, the appearance of the Red Hot Chili Peppers' bassist would have been cause for an uproar. But here in Vegas, the crowd shrugged and raised another glass.

Still, there were highlights, like the inclusion of rarely performed numbers like "You're in Cleveland Today," or the reappearance of Poltz, who sang a spirited "Silver Lining" with his ex-squeeze. But Jewel wanted to finish the show, and the year, as quickly as possible, so she counted down to midnight a full two minutes early. The balloons dropped, and a street scene from the local news appeared on one of the video screens flanking the stage. The graphic said 11:58.

The audience was treated to plastic champagne flutes, containing a swallowful. At one point, a zealous audience member insisted that the singer take a glass from him. She sipped it, turned her back on the audience, and spit it back into the glass. (It couldn't have been a real fan: They all know Jewel doesn't drink.) It seemed like the perfect anticlimax to an anticlimactic evening. Still, Jewel managed to bring the crowd together during a tearful, singalong version of "Foolish Games," which had the crowd swaying as one—even as the piano player, the Rugburns' John Castro, flubbed so badly that Jewel insisted he stop playing. She quickly ran through "Chime Bells," and disappeared into 1998. It was 12:15. A whole year was ahead of her.

Would it—could it—be as incredible as the year that just passed? The world wanted to know: What could Jewel Kilcher do for an encore? "I have different ambitions," she has said. "I wanna do poetry books, write novels, write scripts, and act." She would fulfill at least two of those ambitions that year. HarperCollins paid her a reported $2 million advance—one of the largest ever for a pop star—for a book of poetry and a scrapbook-cum-memoir. The poetry book, *A Night Without Armor*, was released in the spring of 1998, with the memoir to follow that fall. *The New York Post* did the math, and figured out that's about $87,000 for every year of her life.

Absent from the public eye for the early part of 1998, Jewel did a media blitz to promote *Armor*, including a reading from the Virgin Megastore in New York's Times Square that was broadcast live to thirteen other Virgin stores around the world. An online poetry contest was also announced in conjunction with the book's release, with a grand prize of $500 offered. The book was also available as a CD, with eighty-seven tracks. Jewel says she's prepared to face the inevitable criticism of dabbling in a more literary milieu. "That's just part of the job hazard," she said. "I expect failure in my life. If I don't, I'm not being sufficiently challenged."

In that case, Jewel might want to develop a really thick skin, as she also made the transition to acting, following in the footsteps of other crossovers like Madonna, Whitney Houston, and Courtney Love. She was cast as the female lead in a $35 million Fox project called *Ride with the Devil*, directed by Ang Lee, maker of *The Wedding Banquet, The Ice Storm,* and *Sense and Sensibility.* In this Civil War saga, Jewel played Sue Lee Shelley, a frontier woman loved by two men, played by Tobey Maguire and Skeet Ulrich, engaged in fighting on the Kansas-Missouri border. The movie was shot in March 1998, largely in Lawrence, Kansas, and was scheduled for a holiday release. While on location, she sent a message to the Everyday Angels via the Internet. She described acting as "simultaneously the most exhilarating and horrifying endeavor I've undertaken in a while." She said it was difficult to make the transition from musician to actor in a few weeks. Rising at 4:30 A.M. to accommodate the grueling shooting schedule meant crashing early in the evening, which goes "against every shred of musician fiber in me. Oh, the traumas of being a little movie starlet."

But before filming began, she seemed to welcome the change of scenery in her life. "I've grown tired of just performing [music]," Jewel said. "I've always welcomed new challenges." In fact, in a January appearance on *The Tonight Show with Jay Leno,* Jewel lamented the "redundancy" of music. The remark alarmed the faithful Everyday Angels, almost as much as Jewel's joke on the *Rosie O'Donnell Show* in February when she said, "Oh, the problems of us rich white girls now, it's terrible," as she considered what to wear (nothing see-through!) at the 1998 Grammys (she was nominated for Best Female Pop Vocal Performance for "Foolish Games").

Perhaps music was not at the top of Jewel's list of priorities at the beginning of 1998. She "sang" the "Star-Spangled Banner" at January's Super Bowl in San Diego's Qualcomm Stadium before a crowd of 68,000 and a TV audience of one billion. The song was lip-synched, however, and the vocal track started noticeably before Jewel began moving her lips. An NFL spokesman said, "She sang over a track. It was a live microphone, and she sang along with her own voice." But Nedra told the *San Diego Union*'s George Varga, "Jewel requested she be able to sing the anthem live, a cappella. [The NFL] said they were now discouraging artists from doing it live." Meaning, they wanted it lip-synched.

An embarrassing snafu before a billion people? Jewel wasn't fazed.

The following night in Los Angeles, she remarked to a fan, "Ah, it was just a football game." But the snafu may have been a tip-off to turmoil within Jewel's management team, as Nedra became solely responsible for guiding her daughter's career.

Still, Jewel couldn't ever leave music far behind. A mob scene awaited her when she played an intimate show in February at one of her old haunts, Java Joe's in San Diego. Only seventy-five lucky guests got inside for the invitation-only performance, which was filmed as part of the two-hour ABC special, *Where It's At: Rolling Stone's State of the Union*, which aired in May. As fans tried to squeeze into the club through side windows, San Diego police were called in to subdue the crowd. Inside, Jewel previewed new songs, performing mostly unrecorded material, including "Winter Song."

And, while promoting *A Night Without Armor*, Jewel gave a hint of what we could expect from her new album, scheduled for a November 1998 release. She wants her new music to be a counterpoint to the cruelty and callousness of society, she said. "There are things that help me, like meditating or prayer or fairy tales, things that enlighten your imagination and don't just capitalize on fear, so I'd like the album to be like that as well."

Jewel was at L.A.'s Roxy at a record release party for Steve Poltz, arriving immediately after an appearance on the American Music Awards, where she had been nominated for Favorite Female Artist (but lost to Celine Dion).

Poltz was there to headline the show to celebrate the release of his first solo record, *One Left Shoe*, for Mercury Records. Dozens of San Diego Everyday Angels came up for the show, and it wasn't long before Jewel, still in awards-show garb—Helmut Lang leather blazer and black pants—joined Poltz onstage for "Silver Lining," "Old Lover's House," and "I Thought I Saw You Last Night." Though she joked onstage about being a multiplatinum artist while Poltz's Rugburns were only "double tinfoil," she also told the audience about the importance of Poltz's influence on her life and career. "He taught me everything about songwriting," she said.

It was a fitting tribute, and an ironic reversal. Less than five years ago a very different Jewel—or perhaps the same Jewel under very different circumstances—jumped up onstage, reeling from the opportunity to sing along with Poltz and his band. Now, in the midst of a touring and appearance schedule that would send most performers to the hospital for exhaustion, Jewel was giving back to the man who gave her a shot. It was a tearful and heartrending reunion, and Jewel succeeded in making those present see just how grateful she was for her success, and how willing she is to share it with those responsible.

Her champions, and those who simply adore her work, were also present. Jenny Price was there (indeed, she signed Poltz to

Mercury Records), as were Eileen Thompson, her former publicist, and Kris Metzdorf, head of radio promotion at Atlantic. Jewel wouldn't have missed it for the world. She quietly sang along to Poltz's opening song, the album's title track (which she cowrote), from her table in the corner of the club.

Deep in Jewel's heart is a love of music and performance—and a love of the people who seek them. As long as she continues to operate from this heartfelt place as an entertainer, this angel's wings may take her to domains as yet uncharted in the history of popular entertainment. For it has been said that success, like endings, is both surprising and inevitable.